# RESCUED

## A CHRISTIAN COUPLE'S STORY OF ADDICTION

KERRY SAMULAK

ISBN 978-1-64300-778-6 (Paperback)
ISBN 978-1-64300-779-3 (Digital)

All scripture texts are from the New King James Version Study
Bible, Thomas Nelson, Inc. Nashville, TN, copyright 1982.

This is a work of nonfiction. The events and experiences detailed
herein are true and have been faithfully rendered as the author
has remembered them, to the best of her ability. Some names,
identities, and circumstances have been changed in order to protect
the privacy and anonymity of the individuals involved. Some have
vetted the manuscript and have confirmed its rendering of events.

Covenant Books, Inc.
11661 Hwy 707
Murrells Inlet, SC 29576
www.covenantbooks.com

This book is dedicated to all who suffer—especially those who suffer from addiction to substances and the consequential pride. If you feel self-sufficient enough to try to make it on your own, then this book is dedicated to you. If you believe that you can stop your addiction at will—but simply have chosen not to yet—this book is for you. If you consider yourself an exemplary citizen and yes, even a role model, but are caught in the daily defeat of constant humiliation, this book is empathetically dedicated to you. If you are escaping reality of loss and grief by numbing yourself, this book may at first lead you to consider that you may experience even greater loss—*the loss of your best friend, your substance*. As you read, know that hypocrisy has brought you more notice than anything you've ever done. We who have become an example of failure, disdain, and embarrassment (yes, they all do know) need not die in defeat.

# INTRODUCTION

It was a long time ago. I didn't start drinking and turn into an alcoholic. I was an alcoholic who started to drink. That means I am a drunk who doesn't drink anymore. It has to be this way. May I never forget.

I had a dream that propelled me into telling my story. In the dream, I saw a ravine filled with black body bags. At first I thought they were garbage bags, but as I looked, I realized that there was a person inside each bag. Individually each bag had been carefully and purposely dumped into the ravine. Each life had been selectively planned to end this way. These bags contained kind and gifted leaders who were now rendered hopeless and dying. Once confident, they were now beaten by addiction. These dying individuals had been starved of inner belief and self-respect. They were strangling from shame. They no longer believed in the goodness of themselves, mankind, or of God. They were physically traumatized from being poisoned with drugs and alcohol. I saw myself in one of these bags. I heard a voice saying, *Speak and you will live!* I tried to lift my head and call out, but I could barely whisper. Making my voice heard would take perseverance. There was none left. The life or death decision of whether or not to be rescued was in the balance. Even though I was dying, I was too embarrassed to call out. Who would hear? What would they think? Speaking the truth was much too simple. *That would never work!* The urgency to cry out in defeat seemed far too difficult. I just wanted it to be over.

The dream ended before I made the final choice of whether to die or to speak so that I could find the will to live. This book is the outcome of that choice. It is my chance to *speak, and therefore live.* Hopefully, some readers will find that they can speak up about an addiction in order to be restored to life. Denial is our worst enemy. The shame and secrecy of addiction are the first and the final stage of death.

I am alive to tell my story. And telling my story is important— for others and for myself. That is what keeps me from going back to drinking. Most people who drank as I did are not here anymore. I am grateful to be alive. It would have been easier to stay in the body bag. But the many hours of recovery, rehab, gatherings, and prayer are worth it. As a matter of fact it is a healthy, faith-filled, and happy way to live. It gets better and it gets easier but I can't afford any complacency. Alcoholism is always lurking about waiting for an opportunity. That's just it. Addiction doesn't leave. I have to be vigilant in surrender. I have to be proactive in prayer. I have to pay attention. At weddings I have to make sure I do not get the real champagne. It would only take a sip for my crazy brain to be craving and spinning off the deep end again.

My life is good now. The hardest part for me is that I never forget about what I did. Because I drank until insanity, others don't easily forget either. People are very kind. Most have accepted me as *recovered* and many have forgiven my actions. Some have even said I'm courageous. But do they still think of me as fragile or sick? Are they feeling sorry for me? Do some think I should have experienced more consequences sooner? I have to wonder and the reason I have to wonder is because those are the things that I ask myself.

I was told not to worry about what others think. I was told not to think of myself so much. *Think of the needs of others and you'll get better.* Here was the dilemma. Since I drank to escape from feelings of self-consciousness and worthlessness, how could I just stop thinking of myself? *Myself* was the scape goat for the alcoholism. It was a deeply ingrained pattern. I was always stuck on me. *Me thinking* has been an obstacle during these years of recovery. *No one understands me. No one wants to help me. God and everyone are ignoring me.* These examples are only a small part of the mental illness that accompanied my thoughts and motives. The *me thinking* has been one of the most difficult patterns to break. I have come a long way in getting free but

I still have further to go in acquiring healthy, altruistic thinking and unselfish motives.

Could I have prevented this disease? I am told not to think so much about the **coulds**. The remorse is dangerous to my spiritual, emotional health and well-being. By working with many knowledgeable people and professionals, I have been convinced that this disease might have been difficult to prevent. However, it may have been prevented from taking me over so completely if I had been spiritually aware. It's like standing on a beach with your back turned to a tidal wave. The circumstances in me were ripe. I had a brain that craved to feel better. I had a love and drive for escape from reality along with a fearlessness of risk-taking. I was addicted to people pleasing and approval. Those are the things that made a deadly combination in me.

For twelve years, I have been maintaining sobriety and recovery from alcoholism. I've learned that I don't know very much. I do know that there is a severe craving that can only be alleviated by a drink—unless you have achieved some time in sobriety. Even then it calls you back. Drinking helped me forget that I hurt. *But I shouldn't hurt,* I would tell myself. *I have a good life, a good family, a good home, job, amazing kids and husband . . .* Why would anyone want to give up those for drinking? Why would anyone want to disconnect herself from a good life? It never seemed like a choice. Commonsense, discipline and the ability to reason were gone—even in short term sobriety. I call it emotional illness or maybe I should call it a greatly impaired defense mechanism.

From a now-sober perspective, it makes no sense to ruin life-long relationships, and years of hard earned respect with a promising future. I can look back now and see the destruction that others must have seen. It was like bringing in a bulldozer and destroying an entire building along with all the resources, affluence, connections, and hopeful possibilities. The legacy that I might've had was now void. I wasn't even sure that I would have the chance to continue my role as a mother and grandmother. There was little confidence in having a meaningful life again. If I hadn't had some human pillars who gave hope, and a merciful God, I would never have made it back.

A medical definition of alcoholism has brought clarity to my thinking: *Alcoholism is a fatal, progressive, and chronic disease.* This definition gives me a perspective of reality that drives my constant recovery. It allows me no loop holes by which I can bend my thinking to ever justify even one small drink. A medical comparison I've been told about is that I have a life-threatening *allergy* to alcohol. The reaction is unpredictable and yet highly predictable. It is often deadly.

A final well-put phrase that always leaves me with a healthy fear toward this disease is a quote from the Big Book of Alcoholics Anonymous: *Our lack of control leads, in time, to only pitiful and incomprehensible demoralization.*[1*] These thoughts help me maintain the assurance that the physical craving for alcohol could easily be reinstated without vigilant faith and action.

It has become a slow, lifelong work of unraveling the truth. I am working my way back to reality and I think I have finally started to get there. I am ready to share my story with you.

---

[1*] AA Big Book, Fourth Edition, pg. 30

## Kerry's Journal
## Winter 2004

*What is happening? It's not working anymore. Alcohol used to give me the perfect buzz. I used to feel peaceful and confident. Now I blackout and don't remember. I only remember anger. I find myself sleeping on the floor with the dog, or playing my horn at two in the morning, or making hysterical phone calls. Why can't it be like it was before? I can't control it. It's controlling me. Everyone is finding out that I'm an alcoholic but I think I'm beyond caring. I will never give up drinking. Now that the word is out, what do I have to lose? I will keep drinking because I don't ever want to stop. I will keep drinking because it is impossible to stop, even if I wanted to. I'm no longer afraid to die.*

## Rick's Journal
## July, 2003

*So how did it get this bad? When did it get this bad? Drinking used to be fun. She used to be fun. It was something we did on the weekends, sitting on the deck, staying up late talking, drinking a beer or sipping a glass of wine. It was relaxing. It was how we'd unwind. It was something we shared, occasionally. But it's no longer an "us "thing. It's her thing. And occasional is now constant. It's certainly not something we can do in public, nor with friends. What was fun is now embarrassing. What was funny is now irritating. She's erratic, unpredictable, and moody. How did I let it let it get this far? And how do I stop it?*

# CHAPTER 1

# WHY DID I DRINK?

I never saw it coming. That is what addiction counts on. It thrives on unawareness. Unawareness of my own condition led me to a skewed perception of reality. I thought of myself as spiritually fit and mature. How could I be so off? Was I over confident? Maybe. I still looked competent on the outside. However, I was unknowingly deceiving us all. I was tricked into believing I could live in the lie. The lie was that I knew who I was.

Had I ever known who I really was? I had always felt a need to search. Searching for an identity was a difficult and lonely task, especially in childhood. I tried on masks. I tried on the *Attention-Seeking* mask. I tried on the *Helpless* mask. I tried on the *Be Nice to Everyone* mask. I tried on the *It Doesn't Matter What I Want* mask. I found God, and I knew He was good. But the deceiver was also there waiting for me to need more. I needed more because I thought that life was supposed to be comfortable. Nurturing is what the deceiver offered me. A sense of numbness and relief felt nurturing to me.

Drinking felt normal. That is why I didn't see it. It was normal for me to deny what was really happening. I could pretend well. I could pretend to be friendly and caring. I could pretend that I hadn't experienced trauma. I could pretend everything was fine. The uncomfortable things went away. It was more about escape than about deception. I was avoiding hurt and I didn't know it.

One of my favorite things to do as a kid was to pretend I was a bug. I would dress up in green and go out in the back yard. I would carefully select a place in the landscaping where I could live as a bug. As I crawled through the bushes, I kept thinking about how I was blending into the bushes and no one would ever see me. If I stayed in my matching surroundings, would I be found? I hoped not. I wanted to escape being me.

Could it be that I enjoyed the game of being invisible because that is what I was experiencing? Being invisible has its good points. Being invisible meant I could stay myself. I could make giant cardboard wings to wear while jumping from the top of the swing set. No one criticized me. No one said anything. Being invisible meant I could have my own conversations with imaginary purple deer without being interrupted. Blending in was comfortable.

Could it be that I drank because the child in me needed to talk after all? Did the child need to say *I don't want to play that game, I don't want to eat that food, I don't want to wear that dress or go to that party?* Did I drink because the child needed approval? Did the seven-year-old need to be told, *you are not dirty, you are not shameful, it wasn't your fault that this happened?*

One winter night when I was about eight, my brother and sister and I played outside in the snow after dark. They got cold and went inside. I watched through the lighted windows of my home while the rest of our family was inside. I pretended that I was a homeless kid who happened to come across a house that I could possibly enter. It felt strangely comfortable to be an outsider. It fit my inner desires. I wanted to go to the door and introduce myself and start to belong to this family. This was the perfect family for me, I thought. But I pictured myself having a vibrant personality as I was welcomed in. I would be funny and witty. They would laugh with me because I was smart and had good stories to tell. When I went inside, I realized that it would never work out for me to be any other person.

I am not unhappy with my family. They are mostly wonderful, intelligent, well-adjusted people. Not perfect, of course, but in many ways outstanding. So why do I have all these strange perceptions that have given me reasons to want to escape? Things happened to me as a child through circumstances, conversations, and situations that were beyond the control of my family. False beliefs entered into my mind and stayed there, becoming more and more solid over time. I behaved according to these lies for most of my life. My lack of confidence brought outcomes that only solidified my perceptions.

At the age of eighteen, I blamed my strange attraction to alcohol on the fact that they changed the drinking age that year. I could drink at eighteen. It was insane. All of us who hadn't even graduated were becoming legal drinkers! *If the government says I'm okay, then I guess I am okay.*

Suddenly, the frustrations that had always bugged me didn't matter anymore. Grades didn't matter. What others thought didn't matter. Pleasing everyone didn't even matter anymore. I no longer had to say "I'm sorry" to everyone. I had found a formula for living. Why hadn't anyone told me how good it would be to get drunk? The self-consciousness left. Problems left. The fear even left. I didn't know alcohol could make me feel like a different person.

Many people seemed almost apathetic about drinking. They would have only one glass. After an hour and a half, some alcohol remained in that same glass. These *novice drinkers* actually left good alcohol behind! *Didn't they get it?* I wondered how they could be so indifferent about the effects of euphoria that came with drinking. They must be naive. Did they really not know that alcohol was a solution for every negative feeling?

At eighteen, I believed alcoholism was something that happened to stupid people. Maybe their brain couldn't handle alcohol. Mine certainly could. They would end up living on a park bench with a paper bag of cheap vodka. Those poor people might have to beg. They didn't take care of themselves. They probably didn't drink enough water or exercise. I knew better. I would quit long before the park bench thing happened. When my conscience started to prick me and tell me I was going overboard, I looked the other way.

Spiritually, I was fine. I didn't see it as a problem to drink and go to church. I knew lots of good people who drank plenty. Some were even Christians. Eventually, I would slow down my drinking and become like them. Responsible people could drink. I was one of those. But churchy people were ruining my buzz. I would get back to God later.

My senior year was interrupted by my first drink. I never recovered.

Sitting in chemistry class one day, I was startled to hear the teacher say that the fermentation process required to make alcohol was a simple process. I wanted to raise my hand. Now I had a dilemma; I had never once raised my hand to ask or answer a question in chemistry class. It didn't fit my personality or my level of interest. Today I was motivated. I could make my own alcohol. *I wouldn't even need an ID!* I found myself raising my hand. "Is that process in the textbook?" I knew I was probably turning red. The surprised teacher, Mr. White, answered my question. "I believe there is a procedure given for making alcohol through the fermentation process in chapter 12." *Yes!* Apparently I could do a chemistry experiment right at home. *There certainly can't be anything wrong with that!* After class, I found myself in a deep and interesting discussion with a guy who had always repulsed me. I had never spoken to him before, nor would I again most likely, but He was very helpful in giving some pointers about fermentation. A few months later I had some amazingly strong and good tasting wine to share for graduation. The wine was by far the most important thing about that night. I also quickly found better drinking people to hang around with too. No hanging around with people who didn't know how to drink, especially on that important night! Graduation became second to drinking. My whole life soon became second to drinking.

As an adult, I had become wise. I could handle it. An adult finds acceptable, more stressful reasons for drinking; there was marriage, babies, quitting drinking, working on our home, quitting drinking, parenting issues, getting my degree, quitting drinking again, starting a teaching career, church activities, and quitting drinking. My job was a top stress producer. I just had to be careful not to overdo it. I didn't want to be a drunk and a parent. I was too afraid of what would happen. I finally knew that the way I drank wasn't normal.

Christmas of 1999, the avalanche of my drinking life began. All the bottled up stuff gave way. I found myself sitting on the basement floor next to the dirty laundry. At the time I didn't realize the importance of loss. But looking back I see that I was grieving when my children left home. In the same year, three of our four children moved away to college. These major changes in their lives took them further away from home but it also took them further away emotionally. They were busy. They were independent. They were thriving and doing what they were supposed to do. It was traumatic for me that our nineteen-year-old son Peter had chosen a school that was twelve hours away. *Twelve hours!* I refused to decorate the tree. I sat down in the basement next to the dirty laundry for a long time. I just sat there drinking, trying to decide what to do. I couldn't get out the ornaments without everyone home. I would wait until the kids came home to finish trimming the tree even if that meant waiting until Christmas Eve. They had to put their own ornaments on. That is how it always had been. We decorated the tree together. The kids would make the ornaments talk. They would fight over where the ornaments were to be hung. You couldn't put the red deer, Clareece, next to the toy soldiers. The angel with too much makeup and orange hair always brought hysteria because she looked like a hooker. I was stuck thinking about these memories while I downed my tumblers of wine. I couldn't move on.

I had forced myself to stay away from drinking because I knew I had a problem with alcohol. But now, as I realized the loss I felt for my kids, drinking was the only thing I could do to get by. I became hysterical. I had to get numb. It makes sense now. I didn't know how to process the grief. I didn't know it was grief because I wasn't used to feeling that. I always escaped feelings, and this time the feelings were overwhelming.

I couldn't see that I was not facing life. I thought I was merely relieving stress from work and busy-ness. I thought I was just a little sad about my kids leaving home. *Everyone tries to relieve their stress and sadness, don't they?* We are told to lower our stress. We are told to deal with it or it will affect our health and well-being, but alcohol created two worlds. There was the world of oblivion and the world of reality. After spending the evening in a cocoon of euphoria, I would wake up to dread, fear, and condemnation. I would dread facing the day and my blackouts from the night before. Sometimes I would find work that I had either sabotaged or begun with no apparent goal. I would dread facing competent people. I would fear knowing that I was no longer competent. I would both dread and fear my future.

I was tired of faking. All my life, I had been nice to others but not to me. I had made decisions based on what everyone else thought was the right thing or the fun thing. Pleasing others eventually brought major resentment after so many years of putting myself on hold. *Is this what I want? Is this what I was told to want? Is this part of my own beliefs? Is this a goal of mine? Do I feel buried or do I feel freedom and purpose that this is what I was created to do?* I could seldom determine whether my motive was truly to help someone or whether it was a draining and dutiful obligation.

When I drank, I was in charge. I forgot about the pressure of people pleasing. I fled from the expectations of others and I enjoyed it. I was doing something for just me. I was becoming truthful. I was escaping rules that had no meaning for me. But it was vengeful, and my effort to get at others only hurt myself. *I'll show them! They can't tell me what to do!* Rage could be expressed when I drank. Rage had been stuffed inside and now I could let it go! Sometimes I shouted out loud and sometimes the rage stayed in my head but it was always well-expressed.

Pretty soon, the drinking and the rage could not be controlled. They were in charge and I was once again being told what to do. Alcohol told me when to drink, how much to drink, and what to drink. I was told what to rage about, and who should receive the rage. Unfortunately, rage came out on the people with whom I felt the most comfortable. They were my own family members. Lashing out created guilt for the anger that was at the expense of those I loved. Selective memory blocked out most of these episodes. But I can still see myself throwing scissors, putting a hole in a wall, and shoving my bewildered husband. These are things that those crazy people, people with emotional illness would do, but never me. These are things that drove me to further my escape.

Resentment became a fuel to drink. The alcohol began to change my personality again. I was no longer carefree and happy. I began to see everything as getting in my way of drinking. Work was in the way. My kids' evening activities were in the way. Church was definitely in the way. But I had to stay active with those things to hide the drinking. People had begun to recognize my constant, slightly drunken persona. People began to try and help (fix) me. Trying to help consisted of telling me how they knew someone who was instantly delivered from a similar addiction. They told me how easy it was. "I know someone who got hypnotized . . . I know someone who went to special counseling . . . Doesn't your church offer anything for addictions?" There were many opinions. Mostly I heard second hand information that was meant to shame me into getting help.

For a long time, I didn't believe I drank for any other reason than I liked it. Alcohol had become the only thing I enjoyed. I wanted to always be under its influence. When I was told that most of us who are alcoholics have things to escape from, I got angry. *That's not true at all! I drink because I am an alcoholic and that's the only reason.* I actually wanted to defend the position that I only drank because I liked it and I couldn't stop. I did not want to deal with any past issues. Past issues were ridiculous. Why spend the last half of your life trying to fix what happened during the first half? Besides, my life had been good. How could a few little incidents affect my thinking from that point on? I wouldn't just let a few silly words or a manipulative adult bring me down. I was steadier than that. I was smarter than that. Even as a kid, I was well adjusted. I never caused anyone problems. My dad said I was easy to raise. I didn't need to be disciplined more than a few times. Once I put crayons in the globe of a light fixture. They melted and made a beautiful picture. Another time I stood on freshly washed slip covers and peed on purpose. Those were the only two times I remember getting in trouble and neither was a big deal. There were no talks with teachers, principals, or law officials. I didn't have problems. I was fine. I was fine but I didn't like to talk or be around people. I was fine but I was terrified of men because of my step uncle's games. I was fine but ashamed of my body because of words I overheard as a teenager. Am I oversensitive? That is exactly what I thought. Why make a big deal out of little things that took place in five minutes' time? No. I drank because I loved it and I drank because I was an alcoholic.

In my drunken mind, I began what I call *Tomorrow thinking.* Tomorrow I would stop drinking and get help. Tomorrow I would fix things. Tomorrow I would figure out how to quit. *Tomorrow thinking* always continued for another day.

I continued to drink because it was too late to stop. I had become so physically addicted that I could not detox without going to the emergency room. I could have stopped early on before my body was addicted. But once I got beyond that short window of time, which I believe was a *God-ordained opportunity,* the physical addiction completely took over. I had ignored God and now I was begging and pleading with Him to fix this terrible thing. My feet would twitch as my stomach churned and the room spun. The shaking, the tremors, and the sweating were there every morning. That is how I became a morning drinker; *I'll just have a swallow and I'll feel better.*

The point of hopelessness came. Why try to stop anymore? I can't do life sober. I will do life drunk. If I die, I die. Maybe I can keep my job and my relationships, even my Christianity. *Hypocrite? Okay, yeah. I guess I am one. I'll keep it all. If people love me, then they will still love me. If they don't, then too bad. I choose alcohol.* I knew I could die from drinking. My blood alcohol level was getting high. It had been above 0.3 the last few times I had detoxed. I had tried to stop and there was no hope for me. I went to AA and I went to counseling. I went to treatment many times. There was nothing for me at those places. No one could get me to want to stop. I was hopelessly addicted to the lifestyle of hidden freedom.

I can hear the self-pity in my voice as I record these memories. As time went on, self-pity was the main thing that kept me from getting help. I had resolved that I would never receive empathy from anyone but me. That was dangerous. That was my protection. I was the only one who understood. I was the only one who gave me the pity I deserved.

In my drunken mind, I was desperately grabbing for things to blame for my drinking. As long as it wasn't my fault that I drank, I maintained that I was still in charge of myself. *Someone or something has to be to blame and it is certainly not me. It must be . . . my job, my parents, my husband, my church, my old friends, stress, anxiety, the devil, God, embarrassment . . . but it's NOT me.* The reason for drinking had become everything else but me. Everyone and everything had turned on me. I lived with constant and irrational fault finding.

It is clear that I am an alcoholic. It is clear that I have had a disease of the mind. But did I have to drink because I had an alcoholic brain? The true question becomes "**Why did I follow the addiction once I knew I had it?**" I quit a number of times. I kept going back to the alcohol. **Why did I return?** I was wounded and traumatized. I was grieving and hurt. I was stressed out.

Not only that, I was spiritually deceived. I believed I could handle alcohol after all. I was very familiar with prayer, freedom, and faith. But I had become spiritually unaware. I had thought myself to be righteous. I had thought myself to be mature and spiritually gifted. I had even been in church leadership for a number of years. I had thought myself to be an effective parent and a wise teacher. What I didn't see was that I had left the door open in one area of my spiritual walk. Pride—the pride of being self-righteous.

The enemy watches patiently for inroads. He looks for places that we have been overconfident. I pray that my story will be like the sound of an alarm to believers who are on the edge of falling. You may not realize your danger. You may not realize the insidiousness of addiction. You may not realize the faith you place in yourself. You may not realize that you are at a fragile point of choice. If there is an area of your life that you are compromising in small ways, consider yourself warned as you read this story. There are no grey areas or middle ground with this disease.

There is hope for each of us. We can become humbly aware of our true motives. We can become desperately aware of our own realistic circumstances. We can become empowered to seek freedom. We can help others get free. It is my hope that all who are being tempted by addictions will gain truth and courage while hearing my story.

# CHAPTER 2

# CHILDHOOD

W hen I was six, I drank a *Schlitz*. I stole it from beside the chaise lounge on the patio while my dad wasn't looking. He would never have permitted me to have beer. But the wet silver and brown can drew me. I knew it was fizzy because I had listened to it. I had watched the poppy bubbles fly out. Why do I now remember the event so well? The taste was sharp and not sweet. I loved the way it burned but then warmed. I loved the way my brain started to lift off. It only lasted a few minutes. But there it was; the craving to have **more.** I knew I would have more.

When I was six, growing up in our small town was a safe and uncomplicated experience. I was the middle child of three. Jay, Lana and I would line up in birth order and laugh about how we were stair steps. In the car, we always sat in *our row.* Sometimes I would complain that I wanted to sit by the window, but it never happened. The three of us got along well but if there were rivalries or fights, the outcome was always two against one. When it was my turn to be the *one*, I was over sensitive about the many nicknames: "Drawzee, Drawzee! Kerry's a Drawzee because she tries to draw all the attention to herself." That was the day I chased my sister around the house with her baton. *That liar! I never try to get attention!* Permanent gouges were left on the bathroom door where she locked herself in. Would I really have beaten her? I think so. Teasing was my weakness, and my brother and sister knew it.

I was the follower. When Lana devised a pretend play scheme, I always went along with her prescribed role for me. I soon became the main character, Sheryl, who was socially inept. But something else was happening in that role play. I **was** the center of attention! I was also the character who received constant ridicule and rejection. I never asked to switch parts. It was comfortable. I enjoyed the attention and I enjoyed making them laugh. When we played church, I would crawl up the isle during the sermon. When we played store, I would knock down the store display and try to steal stuff. When we played drowning, I would pretend to be the inept rescuer. One day at the beach, a man came running in the water, fully clothed, to help me save my *drowning* sister.

Sheryl was my role for three or four years. Perhaps this added to my feelings of inferiority. Perhaps it didn't. But I was more than comfortable playing the family scapegoat. I was supposed to be both embarrassed and embarrassing. I was supposed to be disliked, offensive and criminal.

Lana was the organizer. She would call *mandatory meetings* at the top of the stairs after we were supposed to be in bed. Each night had a topic.

"Tonight we're each gonna tell about something funny that happened at school."

I hesitated. "I dropped my snack."

"You have to say more, Kerry. What happened then?"

"I don't remember!"

"Is that all you have?" Lana would let out an exasperated sigh. Jay could always find something worthwhile to share about recess or gym class.

Jay, Lana, and I did well in school because that is what we were supposed to do. It became apparent at an early age that learning was easy for them. Everything seemed easy for them. I was the one who sat at the kitchen table with my dad until nine thirty at night trying to understand math. Yes, I received decent grades, but not everything came easy to me. I worked hard.

Things looked backward to me. Bs were Ds, 3s were Es, and left was right. I often missed math problems because I reversed my numbers. This added to my growing feelings about being strangely different. My mother made it a big deal. She talked about it often. *Kerry is left-handed, you know* . . . came up each time I tried something new: sewing, making Valentines, tying my shoes, playing piano.

Because I was a thumb sucker, my front teeth protruded. I was told that I was going to have to wear braces on my teeth in a few years. This seemed exciting to me. I had seen someone wearing a brace around their head at the orthodontist's office. I decided to make my own head gear to wear at school. I made a huge wire contraption that fit around my head and mouth. As soon as I put it on the next morning, the teacher immediately said, "Kerry, what is that wire you have on your head?"

Suddenly I felt all the stares from the class. Turning red, I told her it was an orthodontic headgear. Seeing my discomfort, she approached me. "You could hurt yourself by playing around with wires. I'm taking this away right now."

I was devastated. *How did she figure out it wasn't really an orthodontic device?* I was afraid she would tell my parents, but I don't know if she ever did.

Embarrassment became a thing I tried to avoid after that incident. I hated the feeling of being singled out. I hated being the one who was attracting all the eyes. I hated the hotness that I knew would start creeping up my face. I especially hated hearing, "Oh, your face is so red, Kerry!" I had no reply, just more redness.

School was usually enjoyable. At lunch, kids fought over sitting by me because I would laugh at their jokes and give them my fruit, even though I didn't always want to. If I wanted my fruit, I would make excuses.

"Kerry, can I have your pineapple?"

I shook my head. "Not today. It's got bugs. Ask me tomorrow."

I had lots of friends and would go along with what they wanted to do. When I was asked what to do next, my response was "I don't care, whatever you want." When I was invited to someone's home, I would go out of obligation. I rarely invited them over to my house.

I was different. Being different brought questions that didn't seem to have answers; questions about the worth of unique qualities. I had a first grade friend who was very different than me. She got in trouble for her loud voice and her anger. When I found out her actions were unacceptable, my confusion grew. I tried to stop wanting her friendship, but I was still drawn. Other children, like me, seemed unsure of themselves. I didn't want to be their friend. I wanted friends who lived their feelings honestly. I wanted friends who weren't afraid of people. I wanted friends who only pretended when it was playtime. Deana didn't play at recess though. She had a mission. Her mission was to correct injustices on the playground. Deana was in the middle of every fight. She was usually outcast because of her hot headedness. But Deana was real and I liked that. I couldn't pay the price she paid for her realness. I couldn't stand to be different on purpose. It was Deana's courage I admired. I was invited to her house once and it was that day I developed compassion for her. Deana had no dad or siblings. It was then that I wondered if that was the price she paid for her differences. She had learned things about life that I couldn't learn. She had experiences that I didn't want to have. *Maybe there were reasons why people are the way they are. Maybe people are made themselves by the family they have. Or is it choice?* I couldn't tell as a child which was the cause. Questions and answers continued for me but I knew I wanted to have courage. Even then I knew that fear of people would lead me in a direction I might regret.

My mother tried to encourage me. She often gave suggestions about other children I could befriend or conversations I might initiate. She gently challenged me to reach out to others and push into relationships. *I think Raelynn would like to be invited. Why don't you talk to Mr. Vincent next time? He wanted to know how you liked the game in Sunday school.* I wanted to answer Mr. Vincent but somehow just couldn't. It seemed like there was a big hand over my mouth.

Church attendance was part of our weekly routine without question. As a six-year-old, I hated being expected to go, but when I got to church, I was always excited about all of it, especially the music. We attended vacation bible school in June every summer. The year I turned eight, Lana and I were in the same class. On the last day, the teacher, Mrs. Cook looked at us individually and said, "Would like to pray to ask Jesus into your heart?" I nodded my head. When it was my turn, I shakily said each word of the prayer. It seemed like feelings were coming from my insides and my head was just stopped and waiting. After that, I remember holding my breath to see if Lana was also going to say the prayer. I was greatly relieved when she too, made the decision for Christ. We were linked from then on in a spiritual way. Even though I was a child, there was a marked difference in my faith after that day. When I found myself alone in the backyard, I began to sing praises at the sky while lying out in the grass.

Family vacations were something I always looked forward to because my parents became *leaders of the fun.* One summer we lived on a campground so we could enjoy camping and the lake. Moss Lake campground was crowded with all sorts of diverse people and our family became friends with many of them. My parents didn't seem to notice social class. Even then I recognized that my mom and dad had a gift for meeting new people and pulling them together. We had campfires almost nightly. There were often thirty people or more who pulled their lawn chairs over to join the group. I remember thinking; *how do they just talk and laugh with people that they don't even know? Someday I will be the one who talks to everyone. Someday I will know what to do. Someday things will be easier.*

My parents are wonderful people. An important strength that my parents passed on to us was the value of time and hard work. My mother never sat down except to read the newspaper for a while in the evening. She was constantly doing—and usually doing with others in mind. She gave hours to the church in musical and charitable activities. She taught school for a number of years until she became too exhausted because the work could not be completed to her standards. My dad worked long hours at his own dentistry business and continued to work on our home or in the community after hours. They seemed tireless. Both of them still do volunteer work. We all have gained from their work ethics.

My dad was a joker. I was thrown in the lake wearing my clothes every summer. If my dessert was on the table and my back was turned for even a second, he would hide it from me. He would stick his finger at the perfect spot on our collar bone to cause us to fold up with laughter. He would play board games with us, tell knock, knock jokes and ask who had the smelly feet. He played tricks on the dog, who was a true member of our family. From my dad we learned to enjoy life.

A highlight of summer was when I went to stay at my grandparents' grain farm for a week. The farm was huge and there were many places to hide and to play. There was one particular barn on the farm where we were not supposed to go because it contained dangerous equipment. My cousin David decided that we had to go in there to see why it was off limits. I was torn between pleasing my cousin and telling my grandmother that David was planning to enter the barn. I went along with him, as usual. As we were leaving the barn, I sliced my finger open on a sharp cutting tool. When I sought help from Grandma, she asked where I got the cut. I lied and said that I had received the cut while playing in the sandbox. After getting my finger wrapped up, she took us out to the sandbox to look through all the toys in the sand to find out what could possibly have cut me so terribly. The guilt was unbearable. We must have looked for thirty minutes for a sharp object in the sandbox. That ruined the rest of the week for me because I couldn't bring myself to tell her the truth. I just wanted the dishonest memory to stop playing over and over in my head. *Why hadn't I been able to do the right thing?*

Other families scared me because I didn't know the rules or norms for their houses. One morning, after spending the night at my friend Carol's house, she decided to make French toast for breakfast. She put an assortment of spices and liquids from the cupboard into the milk. As she climbed all over the counters and stove, I thought, *I would never get to do this at my house!* I gagged, and managed to eat half of the sticky rubbery mess. Carol somehow ate it out of sheer determination. I kept thinking that I should tell her mom, but that would be too uncomfortable. I wondered, *Would her mom have cared?*

25

Another friend had a sister with no sense of privacy who would come into the bathroom while I was on the toilet. She kept saying, "Aww, isn't she cute? She's adorable," as she looked at me in the mirror while fixing her hair. I was annoyed but felt that I couldn't say anything. I planned my bathroom trips when she wasn't nearby.

But there was one home where Jay, Lana, and I visited that felt almost comfortable. Our minister, his wife, and their three children were some of my mom and dad's best friends. Their youngest son Chan was my brother's age, and Karen, their middle child, was one of my sister's best friends. That left me to hang out with Melissa, who was a teenager. I always knew Melissa was trying hard to find things to do that I enjoyed. Though we did fun stuff, like painting our nails, I knew she was just being kind. When Melissa had to leave for a high school activity, I quickly became an unwanted addition. Soon I would hear Mrs. Milton say, "Lana and Sharon, you have to play with Kerry now." I always looked down to avoid seeing the silent exchange of bewilderment on Lana and Sharon's faces.

My family was close friends with our neighbors, the Larsen family. I have good memories of the times our family got together with them. All of the kids joined together to put on plays for the adults. At the conclusion we served refreshments. We had cookouts and played *Kick the Can*. Jay, Lana, and I often swam in the Larsen's pool with their children. We played exclusively with these kids because there were no other children on our block. Lana and Jay had playmates Mark and Bonnie with whom they connected. I, once again, was paired with the older sibling, Mimi. Sometimes I would be included in group play where I enjoyed the role of scapegoat. I was the prisoner who was locked in the basement fruit cellar. I was the one who was selected to chase everyone else. I was the one that played the bride while *getting married* to a weird kid from the other block. I was also the one who was dressed up in rags and given a ride down Main Street in the wheelbarrow. I was the gullible one that was taken on a blindfolded, scary pretend trip to hell.

I will never forget the day that Lana, Bonnie, and I discovered a tree that was perfect to climb. We assigned every branch the name of a room. We even made up a song about the tree. I couldn't wait to get to the tree the next day. I, the youngest in the *girl group*, was included in the important play at the tree house.

A few weeks later, Lana and her neighbor friend Bonnie found a new tree to climb. They were up in the tree making their daily play plans. I tried to get up on the first limb but I was just a few inches from grasping it. I spent about ten minutes stretching to reach the limb. It seemed like life or death to me. I was overcome with feelings of loss as I perceived that my sister was stolen from me. I was replaced by Bonnie, the neighbor and I no longer felt needed or important to my sister. I believed that Lana and Bonnie's close relationship meant that I could no longer have the close sisterly relationship that Lana and I had enjoyed. These feelings seem over sensitive, inaccurate, and even petty to me now, but they felt overwhelmingly truthful at the time, and they hurt deeply. This, for me, was the beginning of a new feeling of loneliness that continued even when I wasn't alone. I cried hysterically and ran from the tree to tell on Lana and Bonnie because they had left me out again. I was actually grieving. *I was replaced.* After that I buried the thoughts and feelings. That was my defense. I have never thought of this event again until recently.

When I was eight, I experienced a traumatic event that was devastating and life-changing. A step relative exposed himself during masturbation while attempting to involve my sister and me. I was left with a cold, stiff, numbness that I didn't know what to do about. You certainly don't talk about it as a child. We were told to keep quiet. The main thing I recall is the aftershock. Alone in the bathroom, I cried hysterically. That was the last time I cried for many years. *Why did this happen to me? Should I tell? Did I do this? I'm just deserving of this because I am LESS. I am someone who gets hurt so others can get their way. That is WHO I am.* I buried the feelings deep. I thought the memory would disappear. I thought I would grow up and have the answers someday. I thought adults would have a clean slate of life handed to them.

Much of my childhood was forgotten until I began to purpose-fully recall memories. I had created a system of sorting out events and placing them in categories. The categories consisted of things to remember, things that didn't matter, and things that I pretended did not happen. As I brought the forgotten memories out, I saw an important pattern; those memories that I pretended to forget contained events that still brought me feelings of sadness or shame. Those feelings didn't seem to fit the foggy childhood memories anymore. I had recreated the memories that weren't good in order to protect myself. I had left the feelings behind. But my beliefs about myself had a lot to do with those true memories and the feelings I had hidden away.

Looking back, it seems that life was simple when I was a child. Somehow I made it complex. Things were bright on the surface. But I was a rider, not a driver. Was I ill prepared for life? I was a kid. I wasn't supposed to feel confident. So was I created with this temperament? I was often deemed the *quiet one*. On the inside I was full of questions and unstated opinions. I do not claim there to be anyone or anything at fault. Exactly the opposite; there is no one to blame. I don't blame God. Nor do I blame my parents, teachers, church, siblings or friends. There are pathways of choice and I took the one that fit. It was comfortable and it was me. I could sense that others would take different roads but neither is right or wrong. Through my adult eyes, I ponder; as a follower, I didn't feel valued. I don't feel any resentment or *what ifs*. But I do wonder. Would the stolen sips of beer have been so fulfilling at the age of six if I had been true to myself? If I had demanded to be heard, to be known, would I have felt less need to escape life? My conclusion is this: I am me. If I could live childhood over, I would change only a handful of circumstances. Overall, I would change very little.

# CHAPTER
## 3

# TEENAGE YEARS

I look at my teen years and think, *Who was I? What did I do that for?* Sometimes the reality is, *I can't believe I did that!* It was the seventies and it truly was a time of *finding yourself.* I actually lost myself in the cliques. Belonging to all of the groups and yet not fully committing to any would best describe me. I was on the edge of smart so I could be on the low end of the studious crowd. I was also on the edge of athleticism during the year that girls' sports were just beginning. Running turned out to be my favorite. Along with my brother, I belonged to the track team and the winter running club. Music was where I had some potential so I threw myself in with the totally unpredictable band crowd. That group fought like siblings because of the long hours spent together on trips. I wasn't even near the edge of the *Do Gooders* clique. That didn't matter. These students accepted me because I got involved in community service projects through my mother's impressive group connections. Eventually, I became interested in the pothead group. Now that was a fit. I was more than on the edge of that one. I was all in.

It is predictable that I constantly worried about what my peers thought of me. I didn't gain self-confidence as I went through my high school years. Getting along with everyone and steering clear of all confrontation were my two frantic obsessions. I was driven to look good in the eyes of others; even when my actions were bad. One of those irreversible actions was when I joined in with a group of streakers on a dare.

Because I didn't know myself, I thought I wanted to be a cheerleader. I first tried out for the cheer team in the eighth grade. Lana easily made the team every year. I overheard my mom ask Lana to help me make up a cheer for tryouts. "Can't you help Kerry? She doesn't know what to do." Lana did help but I never was sure if she wanted to. Lana made up a fantastic cheer with wonderful rhythm and motion for me to perform at tryouts. When I went out on the gym floor to perform it, I froze. I couldn't remember any of it. I stood there turning red, lost in embarrassment and frustration for at least a minute. Finally the coach said. "It's okay, Kerry. Maybe you'll remember in a few minutes." I never did get it right. After trying a second time, the cheer came out all mixed up. I tried out for cheerleading every year after that but didn't make the team. Finally, in my senior year, I made the team only to find that I hated being in front of a crowd of people. I was so self-conscious that I never really did enjoy cheering. Belonging to the cheer team and being thought of as *cool* were the important things for me.

I continued to have lots of friends as I went through high school. Friendship seemed easy for me because I was a follower. Others always made the decisions and I would be the one to go along. One of my friends invited me to the movies one Friday night. The bank was closed so I couldn't cash my A&W check. There was no ATM in 1972. No one was home to borrow from. I used my two silver dollars that my grandfather had given me from the 1930s to pay admission to the movies. I had been advised never to spend those coins but the important thing that evening was that I go along with my friend because she asked me to. I always seemed to be living for the moment with no thought of future events.

My favorite thing in high school was playing the French horn in band. Not only did I enjoy the musical experience, but there were many fun trips and activities. The mix of all the classes in grades nine through twelve was interesting. My sister was also in band and she made it even more fun. Lana, who could've been a comedian, would imitate the band director with unbelievable accuracy. She would even catch my attention during band class and mouth familiar dialogue to me. She was a clown and everyone appreciated her humor. Some of us got in trouble while laughing at her jokes during practice.

On one of the band trips, we were at a restaurant for breakfast. When I tipped a bottle of syrup upside down to squeeze, the cap came off and the syrup poured down the sleeves of my uniform. There was no choice but to continue to wear the jacket since we had to remain in uniform for the performance. I hated the attention that I received from this experience. Everyone was talking about it. "Did you see what happened to Kerry? That was so cool! We couldn't stop laughing." I viewed this episode as an opportunity to believe my already poor self-image. *This wouldn't happen to anyone else. How could I be so stupid? Wearing this sticky jacket fits my weirdness.*

Math was my least favorite subject, and I was even a little scared of it. Maybe that was because the teacher was moody. Mr. Allen was also the basketball coach and every Friday was a sober, intense class. We would remain quiet and work on homework after we took our weekly test. On Monday, if the team lost, we knew better than to talk or laugh. Mr. Allen would be angry and sullen. I saw him grab noncompliant boys by the collar a number of times.

He wouldn't even greet the class on those Mondays. He would simply come in and start placing the graded tests on each desk. He would place them in order of percentage correct. The first row was where the same five honor students were always placed. The remainder of the class stood nervously as each name was called, and our test was placed on a seat. Obviously, everyone knew the rank order of each student. More than once, I was placed in the next to the last row, and one time, I achieved the last row. That was a humiliating week. It proved to be more difficult to learn when you were concentrating on how you would look to the rest of the class. I was also distracted while learning because I worried about my placement the following week. Appearance was always most important to me. When the basketball team won, Mr. Allen would sometimes even smile while telling interesting, off-topic stories. That did not change how I felt about Mr. Allen or about math.

Boyfriends were a problem. I had one major relationship all through high school. We would go together and then he would dump me for a few months to date others. After dating others we would get back together for a while. These breakups were very difficult for me. I felt major rejection each time. However, I felt in love and I didn't care that I kept getting used and dumped.

I dated some other guys but it wasn't the same. I never wanted to hurt feelings so I would go out with boys that I liked as friends, knowing that they considered it more. I didn't even think about their well-being or feelings. Self-centered fear was my driving force and the fear of being alone always seemed to win.

One night, I had made plans with Dennis but another boyfriend called and asked me to go out at an earlier time. I went on the date that was planned at the last minute, knowing that Dennis would be showing up just before I got back. I just shoved it aside in my head and pretended it wasn't happening. When we returned, Dennis was waiting in his car in front of my house. He began to yell and make a scene that all the neighbors could hear. I couldn't stand the confrontation or the conflict. My friend James went right home but Dennis stayed and accused me of cheating on him. I was relieved but saddened when my dad came outside and asked Dennis to leave. "Go on home if you can't act in a civilized manner," Dad said. To my surprise, Dennis left while screeching his tires down the street. I still remember my sister's words and her nickname for me as I came in the house that night; "Real good, Gurnz! What'd you do that for?"

*Why did I go on a date when I knew that I already had made plans?* Those were my thoughts as I tried to go to sleep that night. I couldn't seem to turn people down when I was asked do things. Being left with no date was worse for me than experiencing the awkwardness of having two people show up. This actually happened two more times in the next several years with different guys each time. I wanted so badly to have meaningful relationships but was unable to make plans or decisions that would bring about healthy, long-term involvement.

During one of these break-ups Dennis dated a girl who was a beauty queen for the entire region of the state. One day, while waiting in my car at the high school for my sister, Dennis and the beauty queen walked out of the high school hand in hand. My already weak self-image took a complete dive and I became physically ill. I broke out in fever blisters and couldn't eat. I wanted to die.

A good friend of mine turned eighteen soon after this. That was the year that the laws were changed and eighteen-year-olds could drink. It was the Vietnam War years. "If they're old enough to fight, they're old enough to drink." My friend Jane went and bought some cheap apple-flavored wine to celebrate her birthday. She asked me to drink it with her. We were driving around with the bottle. She took a swig and passed it to me. As soon as it got to my stomach, I felt the same warm buzz that I had experienced when I tasted open beer as a six-year-old. I had to have more. I couldn't stop drinking the wine. When the bottle was gone, I asked her if she wanted to get more. I was just getting started. She was starting to feel sick so she was finished. I felt like I was starving for the alcohol. Nothing else was important at that moment, not even Dennis.

During the months that followed, I drank whenever possible. I would steal it from my parents' cupboard or find other seniors who were already eighteen. For the rest of that year, I even started to drink at inappropriate times, like before a night of cheerleading or a dance. Amazingly I didn't get caught and I was able to function quite well with a good buzz on. I seemed to have tolerance that others didn't. I made sure that alcohol was a major part of graduation celebrations. My classmates were amused that I always went to extra lengths to get it. I would plan the drinks several days before an event. The week after graduation, I crossed over to hard liquor. No one realized how important the alcohol had become to me, including me.

There was a change in my friends at this time. I began to hang around with party people. I started dating a drug dealer. It felt like a new life had begun for me. I could relax. This guy, Bart was so much nicer to me than Dennis had ever been. Another girlfriend who I had never cared for became my best friend. There was a large group who were all into smoking pot. I enjoyed pot, but still preferred the alcohol.

There were many parties after graduation. One night I was playing Frisbee while drunk. I fell into some landscape timbers. My reflexes were so slow that I didn't catch myself. The bridge of my nose crashed into the corner of a timber. I had a bad cut that bled for a while. I was not the least bit concerned and neither were my friends. As a matter of fact, we laughed. It could've been fatal but I was oblivious. I believe that God was watching out for me, even in my drunken state. I do still have a scar that helps me remember what alcohol can do.

The summer was a blur of fun. I did nothing but work and party. I had self-confidence again. I liked myself again. It seemed like I had a new personality and I was even funny. Instead of catering to people, I was their equal. That is how the alcohol began to be so necessary to me. It bolstered my self-confidence and made me feel acceptable.

# CHAPTER
4

# COLLEGE

In the fall of 1974, I attended MSU. I wasn't sure I belonged at college, but there didn't seem to be any options. That is what we did in my family; we went to college. Unfortunately, I had chosen a major university with all kinds of choices. For me that was a problem. The university was big and overwhelming. I didn't even have a major because I couldn't decide. That was a glimpse of my state. Indecisive. I couldn't choose anything so I let it choose me. A large university is not a place to let your life choose you. I came from a small town. I had experienced a sheltered, conservative, and less complicated way of life as compared to students from large cities and modern households. There had not been many choices to make. My school, friends, or parents had made all my choices for me up to this point. This sounds like a predictably problematic situation. It was.

As I got out of the car at my dormitory that first day, I heard a unique giggle. I looked up and saw another nervous young freshman woman. "Did you say you were in room 238? You're my roomie!" she blurted at me. This was a huge relief to me. *She's friendly!* We bonded immediately, like kindergarteners do on the first day when they find a friend. It turned out that we were compatible roommates. Karen, too, had led somewhat of a sheltered life and was raised in a family similar to mine.

Karen had a friend who enrolled late. They were hoping to room together but Karen had already been assigned as my roommate. Over that first week, Karen's friend Martha gradually began to move her things into our room. She soon declared, "Let's see if we can live here as a trio. There's enough space for three in this room. The university won't care because they're over crowded anyway." Now here was a decision maker. I welcomed her as a friend because Martha also liked to party. She was bold, charismatic, and smooth. She became well known throughout the dorm. Everyone was amazed that the three of us had voluntarily decided to share a room together. Karen was highly disciplined. She would go off and study for long hours. Martha and I always found somewhere to party or something else fun to do.

Alcohol was easily accessible. I was introduced to trash can parties. People would bring whatever booze they chose and dump it into the trash can. This started during *Welcome Week* but extended into the term. Weekends were crazy with parties. If you wanted to escape drinking parties, you had to make a point of leaving and going somewhere else. A few of us continued to drink all week. I couldn't stop on Monday. The craving was too strong and I couldn't face the scariness of college. I needed the confidence and the euphoric assurance that the alcohol provided.

I thought of myself as mature for my age and well prepared for life beyond high school. Alcohol intensified these beliefs. Having a drink became my solution for all of the unknowns I was facing as I entered college. Having a drink became my solution for feeling socially successful. Having a drink covered all the fears that were quickly piling up. During the hangover times, I was lost. I didn't feel like I belonged anywhere when I was sober. Socializing became difficult. Carrying on conversations became a series of awkward gaps while sober. When drinking, I managed to carry on plenty of conversations. Sometimes the talking turned into attention seeking lies. One night at a party I told a story about how I had sprained my ankle by performing difficult dance moves. The truth was that I had sprained my ankle by missing a curb in my drunkenness. There were others at the party that knew dance moves and wanted to know more about my dancing. The friends I came with knew the truth. They were laughing uncontrollably. This was one time that I realized alcohol had brought complication instead of solution to my success.

Somehow, I managed to get good grades my first term. That only gave me false assurance that I was okay. My parents were pleased, too. I had survived and I still looked good. *I can do this!*

Winter term I discovered you could put a six-pack out on your window ledge to keep it cold. More than once, snowballs were pelted at our second story window by students who were trying to steal my stash. I became a daily drinker and I failed several of my classes. "You should cut back on your drinking," Karen said to me. I wasn't ready to hear that. *She is never any fun.* That was my resentful conclusion. I don't think I realized that *drunk* was my new normal.

In the spring, though Martha and I were on academic probation, the three of us planned to sign up as suite mates in a new coed dorm for the next fall. We sought out a friend who was also looking for a new roommate. She agreed to room with me. The four of us went to sign up for the new, popular dormitory across campus. There were many applicants and few openings for Wendell Hall. We camped out overnight on the steps of the housing office so that we would be first in line in the morning. I was surprised to see that there were several other groups who had the same idea. There were about eighteen people camped out in the stairwell for the night. It was an almost magical time. All night we told stories, laughed, sang, even danced. After that, many of us who met that night continued to socialize. My husband, Rick was one of those people on the stairway. We immediately bonded, but we didn't date right away. I started dating Dennis again over the summer.

That summer after my freshman year was a blur of working, drinking, and weekend parties. There were friends at my family's lake home who enjoyed excessive drinking as much as me. On week nights, I drank on my own. The Chicago friends went home to work and returned every Friday. My old drug dealer boyfriend, Bart showed up for a while. That gave me incentive to believe that I was doing alright. I looked much better than him. He could barely keep a job. This again gave me false energy to continue the lie of drinking.

In the fall, the new dorm proved to be very socially driven. It was easy to meet people. There became a larger group of people who added to the number from the stairwell group. One of the guys who was especially influential had a religious experience. He, in turn began to lead others to Christ. They started having meetings and bible studies. *What? At college?*

This perplexed me. How did I fit into this? I could see they were happy and in a much better place spiritually, emotionally, and even academically. They weren't partying. I was drawn to them and to God. There was a small seed of truth there that I couldn't excuse. They had freedom. I had been a church goer all my life but those things didn't mesh with drinking or the party life-style. Religion was for kids and old people. I knew that I would never give up drinking. I tried to live on both sides of the fence. I would go to their spiritual gatherings but I still drank. Sometimes I even went to these meetings under the influence of alcohol. Now I was seeing another thing that I couldn't stand about myself; extreme hypocrisy. That only made me drink more. It became an obsession in my thoughts. *I thought I loved God too, but I can't give up alcohol for Him. Why can't I be like everyone else and just drink on the weekends? I seem to be the only one who has SIN!*

I was unable to make decisions because there were always two or more opinions and conflicting answers to my academic troubles. Martha had major hatred for the *God people*. "They're Piss ants! C'mon, I know where there is free booze." Another close friend kept repeating, "Wow man, are you ever screwed up. Relax. Have some pot." There were several caring friends cheering me on, "You gotta make some tough choices here but you can do this . . . Do you even have a major yet? You gotta start studying and quit partying." And what was I saying to myself? *You're gonna flunk out. What're you gonna do then? I just wanna quit and drink.*

Finally, I woke up early one morning just before exams in a stupor. What day was this? Or was it night? I was wearing the same clothes that I had on yesterday. *I think that was yesterday.* I had tried to study but I couldn't think with or without a buzz. *Were my finals this week?* These thoughts scared me enough to pull things together for that semester.

Then summer was here again.

Welcome week and fall of junior year were here. I was glad to be on my own again after living at home for the summer. It was getting harder to pull off sobriety at home.

At school, I left off where I started except for one thing; I was dating my future husband. After being friends for a year, Rick and I had started getting serious. I had stopped dating guys who were not interested in me for me. For once I had made a choice for my good.

Rick had no idea how much I drank. I could still behave in a fairly normal way while being under the influence and I was drinking more and more in secret.

October 18, 1976, is a monumental day in my life. My life changed forever that day. I was sitting in a booth across from Rick in a downtown grill. "A Coke? How can you ask me if I want a Coke right now?" I was numb. I felt like I had just witnessed a huge crime. I was shaking. Reality had hit me in the face. I needed to escape. I had to get out of this but there was no escape. I was pregnant. The doctor at the health center had shook his head and looked at me with compassion and worry. "I don't know what to tell you. I have a daughter myself and I know this must be very difficult. I wish I could give you better answers."

Rick and I both knew that we wanted to get married. He officially proposed and we began the huge and uncertain process of planning a wedding, marriage, and birth. The very hardest thing was telling our parents. We planned what we would say and how we would tell them. We decided to go together to be a united front. He would tell his parents and I, mine. I still remember almost word for word what we decided to say. The script went like this; "We have important news. We are engaged and planning to get married in December. We are also having a baby in June."

We told his parents first. They both cried but his mother saw our pain and panic. She immediately turned her attention to the joy of the situation: "How wonderful! I'm so happy for you!" His dad focused on the practical: "What about school? I'll keep paying your tuition. Have you looked for a job Rick? I don't want you quitting school. Kerry could live with her parents while you finish your degree." *What? That cannot happen!*

Telling my mom and dad was the most dreadful thing I had ever done. The air was tense and full of unsaid words during the long silence. They had mixed expressions of concern, loss, and resignation. They only asked a few questions. Would I finish school? Where would we live? We began to plan the wedding with them right away; even amidst the still resentful atmosphere. The time-line was short and now I realize how hard my parents worked to make it all happen. I know I couldn't have done what they did.

Again my friends were split in their responses: "What are you thinking? You're not **really** going to marry this religious guy, are you? What about Dennis? You still love him. I know you do." The other side attempted again to remain positive and upbeat; "You two will make it work. Look at the future. A baby! Wow! . . . and what will the wedding be like?" There were those of the church crowd who surprised us with second-hand shunning remarks; "Kerry and Rick are in sin. Don't fellowship with them. They have consequences to live out." Although all these remarks and opinions cut me deeply, I had to let them be. I was still too weak, sick, and shocked to try and make peace or explain myself. Rick got a part time job that same week and we had little time together between school, work, and wedding planning.

I stayed numb for several weeks. My legs were barely supporting me. I ate very little and was starting to throw up. I was so worried about what everyone else thought or said that I didn't even process what I felt except that I was scared. That fear came loudly through the fog of mixed voices. Gradually, it gave way to shame and self-hatred intermingled with the fear. *I'm a definite loser*, I thought. I was being forced to face reality and responsibility for almost the first time in my life.

One important and insurmountable thing had happened in those two weeks. I had stopped drinking! I had been shocked into sobriety. And though I felt that loss, there was little time or energy to give way to it. I made an OB appointment and started to pay attention to my health.

The alcoholism was behind me now. I was sure of that.

Our wedding day came quickly and the ceremony was amazing. It was a Christmastime candlelight service at the church where I had grown up. We received comments for several years about the wedding. People felt *something*. A few even said they experienced God's presence. It really did seem like I had momentarily dropped off my stressful self and picked up a new perspective. There was some peace because I had made a good choice and intuitively knew it. Since we immediately moved into married housing, I wasn't as available to those who had pulled me around with constant opinions. The party people disappeared.

The weeks passed in a whirlwind. Soon it was June and our daughter Samantha was born. Becoming a parent felt like the doorway to a new life. Nothing was the same again. I wasn't prepared for the long hours of giving. And yet Samantha was so worth it. I wanted to just be a parent and stay home but given our financial situation that wasn't possible. I went to work as a waitress, something I knew well, while Rick finished school and completed his internship. My parents offered me tuition money, but I couldn't fit school into my life anymore. Besides, I had not been able to find a major that truly interested me. My life had taken a sharp turn.

# CHAPTER
## 5

# MARRIAGE

The man I married is the man that was divinely selected for me. I really believe that. There are character qualities, convictions, and drives in Rick which eventually inspired my beliefs and my choices. I knew I could find the right direction for me. But I had to want that direction. That took time. Our marriage survived the consequences of a wrong turn.

Marriage was hard work. We had little time to adapt to building our relationship before we became parents. Neither Rick nor I were ready for the unselfishness required of parenting. At first, child discipline consisted of the authoritarian, *Because I said so* response. I felt like I was constantly giving, but on the inside, I was wishing I had more to give. I felt like a squeezed out sponge—with no chance for getting my own needs met. And I had many needs. I think I was still emotionally a teenager. Learning to parent took patience and self-control, which I had little of. Lack of sleep was a true test. Early morning yelling fits, for which I am ashamed to admit, were a normal occurrence. The saving grace was that we were blessed with an extraordinary firstborn child who didn't heavily try our parental expertise. Our second daughter, Kylie, was born shortly after Rick got his first teaching position. She was an adorable, bright, lively baby who required constant chasing. We frantically called poison control several times during her terribly curious second year.

It seemed that no matter how hard we worked in those early years, there was an ever-mounting pile of unfinished daily tasks. We rarely sat down. Rick did dishes, gave baths, changed diapers, and read with the kids at night. He was also teaching a night class and attending graduate classes. I was overwhelmed with the demands of toddlers and household tasks. Sometimes it was three o'clock in the afternoon before I got my own teeth brushed.

Rick and I were still best friends, much like we had started out in college. A busy life took over. We settled into having our family and enjoying them. Our two sons were born before we reached the age of thirty. Part of my birthday gift that year was a nap. By that time, we had learned that children, for us, were worth the sacrifices of parenting. Their value was much more important to us than careers or money in the bank. They were the ones with whom we loved to spend our time. They were my life.

Since I wanted to stay at home while the children were young, Rick and I agreed that our budget would have to be seriously stretched. Could we even live on a salary of eighteen thousand dollars? That would require more than simple discipline and living in a frugal manner. We purchased our first home for only sixteen thousand dollars. I joined a food co-op, made clothes, curtains, and food from scratch. I planted a garden and bought many of our needed items at garage sales.

For vacations, our family of six would all cram together in one tent to go camping. It was our goal to see how many fun things we could find to do that were either free or had little cost. We found many cheap activities; tubing on the river with free, patched up tubes, hiking and biking—even in the rain with ponchos that cost one dollar, rock skipping contests, park ranger role play, games, sand castles, body surfing, nature collections, campfire cooking, scouring the woods for the perfect hot dog stick, and, of course, staying restaurant-free.

We joined a church that was small and close knit. We had friends who pitched in and relied on one other. I could trade babysitting favors. It was at this church that I learned that God was real and that I was loved even if I didn't feel worth being loved. Both people and God were showing me unconditional love. It seems like I started to grow up and become an adult during those years.

I began to parent with more patience and empathy. I was able to feel for my kids when they had difficulties. I wanted them to have friends and to enjoy many types of activities. That meant going out of my way to drop off, pick up, and constantly provide. I was fortunate to have several close friends who kept me steady and in touch with the adult world.

During these years of early marriage, there was no time, space, or money for drinking alcohol. These were the years that I drank very little. However, if we went to a wedding, reunion, or a party with free alcohol, I downed as many drinks as possible—and as quickly as possible. The craving immediately returned as soon as I had my first sip; even after years of dormancy. It felt like I was transported to another era. I have later learned that this is called binge drinking and it is what alcoholics often do.

We went to a family gathering one weekend and I drank heavily. I had hidden drinks around my parents' house at different locations. When it was time to go home, I panicked. *Where did I put all of those glasses? There will be no alcohol tomorrow. Should I try and take some beer with me?* Rick kept pestering me to leave and I kept making excuses to stay so that I could go and drain down the remaining beers. It didn't matter to me that it was past the kids' bedtime and Rick had to work the next day. My priorities changed when I drank. When we got in the car, I passed out for a while. When I woke up, I was already feeling the uneasiness of the alcohol being removed. I began to pick a fight with Rick. "I don't know why you were in such a hurry to leave," I said. "We hardly ever see my family," which wasn't true at all. When we got home, I threw a child's wooden chair across the room and broke it. I was ashamed and blamed it on the stress of being with extended family all weekend. Now I can clearly see that the anger was from withdrawal. I didn't drink again for a number of years.

As the kids grew, they became more and more involved with sports and musical activities at school. Every night there was something to attend. These years flew by and are now kind of a blur to me, even though I enjoyed them very much. I went back to college and earned my teaching degree. I had finally made a decision about a career. Being a teacher was something that, in my college years, I never even considered. Teaching had now become a deep desire. At first, I only took one class at a time because it just seemed too overwhelming, and yet, I wanted to hurry and finish. We needed the second income. I finally graduated in 1992 and started teaching part time in 1994.

The church frowned on drinking so we did very little of it. One New Year's eve, Rick had surprised me with a bottle of wine to share when we returned from our evening out. We were invited to get together with friends from our church. I decided not to go because I wanted to stay home and drink the wine. I talked Rick into staying home. When the bottle was empty, I insisted on getting more. One bottle wasn't nearly enough. "You better get two bottles. It's New Year's!" The next day, I needed more. The craving was overwhelming. I drove to the store and bought more, even though my tight grocery budget did not allow for it. Eventually, the end of the *drunk buzz* still came and I felt the loss strongly.

This was the beginning of the short time frame in which Rick and I drank together. He was only a social drinker. He grew up with alcohol being a small part of social events. Having beer or wine occasionally was normal for him. He still assumed that I, too, was a social drinker. It was easy for me to look responsible and drink wine on weekends. For a while this worked out nicely. I could justify my need for alcohol because, since Rick was drinking along with me, I was not drinking alone. *Drinking at home with your spouse is normal.* To add to the acceptance, we had changed churches and were now attending a fellowship where drinking alcohol in moderation had always been allowed. They viewed it as a continuation of the practice of taking small amounts of wine during the early Christian faith. *So I'm not doing anything wrong after all!*

My drinking escalated quickly after I began full-time teaching at the public school. The stress was overwhelming. I could use that as an excuse for drinking. I looked forward to Fridays when I could drink. It seemed to relieve the stress and provide escape from worries. I was unprepared for the many hours or the huge responsibility of teaching while assuming my role as a mother. That was my justification to escape to the relief of a nightly buzz.

At my suggestion, we started to buy boxes of wine on Fridays because it was more economical. This meant that I could drink a lot more without the specific amount being noticed. No accountability. That is what an alcoholic desires most.

It wasn't long before I had to buy a second box to get through the weekend. I didn't want Rick to know that I was drinking most of the box so I would buy more wine and replace the box. I hid the boxes in my bedroom because I didn't want the kids to know that I was drinking large quantities. Although, I think they were starting to become aware. The kids were in high school, so they were well aware of the changes in my behavior. There were often five or six boxes under the bed. I would dispose of these when no one was home to see the number.

The boxes of wine started to stretch into Monday because Monday was unbearable. Going to work on Monday with a craving and a hangover was too difficult. Now I look back and remember that I thought drinking was helpful. *You have to learn to relax when you are under this much stress.* Monday morning was simply the price one had to pay for the weekend enjoyment. If the box wasn't empty on Monday, then Tuesday is when I would finish the box . . . then Wednesday.

I knew I was in trouble and I knew I was an alcoholic. For some, knowledge is all it takes to get out of alcoholism. Admitting that you have a problem is the first step in the twelve step programs. I had a choice then. I could've stopped drinking. I chose to continue. There were, however, times when I told Rick that maybe we should slow down on the drinking. I wanted to see if I could control my drinking. He didn't know yet how much I was drinking so he didn't see any problem. He agreed to only drink on weekends, which he had mostly been doing anyway. It worked for a short time but then I didn't hold up my end of the agreement. I began to make sure that I always had wine available. It was quickly becoming number one in my life. I began to make all of my plans based on when and how I could drink that day.

The sneaking is what really made me take a nose dive into hard drinking. The deception is a downward spiral. Once I started to deceive others, I was also deceiving myself into believing that I was still okay. Drunkenness was now becoming routine, even on week nights. *Lots of people drink every day, right? Especially wine. Priests drink wine. Wine is the drink that Jesus made for a wedding and His wine was the best tasting stuff!* Those were my thoughts of justification. The idea that I could stop drinking was now buried under complete denial.

I prayed every day. I asked for forgiveness for drinking so much. I asked for help to drink less. These episodes of prayer were usually during the early morning hangover when sweats, shaking, nausea, and diarrhea were routine.

I knew that God was still there. He told me that He would give me the strength to stop. God never left me, but in my mind I knew I was a hypocrite. I wanted to be a functioning alcoholic, I wanted to be a committed Christian, and I wanted more years to drink. I wanted it all. The double standard brought even more incentive to escape.

In 1997, losses were starting to occur because of alcohol. Relationships were beginning to suffer. Trust was disappearing from our marriage. Criticism and anger became normal interactions at home. I no longer reached out socially. I had stopped growing spiritually, emotionally, and personally. I was *off the path*.

# CHAPTER
## 6

# THE FIRST YEARS

During the first few years of daily drinking, I gradually became both psychologically and emotionally addicted to alcohol. I couldn't wait to get home to drink. Even though I still believed I could stop if I wanted to, I depended on the relief from stress and worry. Teaching, like parenting, was a depleting and exhausting job. I loved it but I hated it. Now I was giving even more of myself and I didn't know which *self* I could trust—the drunk or the sober. I think I was also addicted to *being needed*. I was constantly meeting demands and giving help to my students or my own children. My two desires—the alcohol and the *being needed*—were fueling me and working against each other. One escalated my requirement for the other.

Our youngest children, Peter and Nolan, were in high school when I started to wonder if I could stop drinking. Because our children were involved in school and church activities, we were gone from home many evenings. Often there were several things to attend. Rick and I would split up and attend separate events so that we could manage everything. This meant that I would have to find ways to drink and still be in a *drivable* state. I worked to maintain the appearance of normalcy. I would drink my two tumblers of wine before dinner and have the third or fourth after I got home from their activities. I believed that my plan was working. I used mouthwash and mints by the pack to try and cover the alcohol on my breath. It didn't occur to me to wait until I got home for the evening to start drinking; that was unthinkable.

Our daughters, Samantha and Kylie, were in college. Although Kylie still lived at home, and Samantha was only an hour away, I found myself secretly regretting their independence. Now I was no longer needed, and that brought feelings of loss. The girls' teenage years had been a whirlwind of busy-ness. I could never say no. I found myself over extended with less important things like fundraisers, volunteer work, and bake sales. I believed that I had failed them. Regret and loss increased my need for drinking.

My personality, like that of many alcoholics, changed when I drank. During this time, I was on a happy high. I became very outgoing, which is unlike my natural tendency. We went to a sports banquet one evening. We sat near a family that we didn't know very well. By the end of the banquet, we were chatting like best friends—at least in my mind. Conversation had become fun and easy. The trouble was that later when I saw this family again, I couldn't reconnect because I was ashamed and because I couldn't quite remember how the situation had ended. *Had someone asked me to quiet down to hear the speaker again? Did they know? I think I was in control that night. I wish I could remember what I said.* Those thoughts got shoved away to deal with later. Those thoughts would offer unwanted proof that I was drinking too much.

I truly believed it **was** working. I was able to drink and still function normally. I thought I would be able to continue this forever. I had found a solution for the difficulties in life. This was it. There was no longer self-consciousness, fear, or stress because I had alcohol. There was energy for everything now.

We went to a Euchre tournament at our church one Friday night. I had already finished my three tumblers of wine before we left and was into my fourth because this was **Friday, the weekend.** It was more difficult to play the game. I had to think hard and I kept forgetting what card was trump. Rick was my partner so it was do-able because he could more than make up for my mistakes. I was talking so much, though, and taking so long that our table partners had to keep saying, "C'mon, Kerry, let's play." I laughed so hard that I started to fall out of my chair. I glanced up and saw Danielle looking at me from across the room. As I started to play again, I noticed she was still watching me. *Was she staring?* Yes, she was. *Did she know?* Probably. I felt exposed but it only lasted for a minute. Selective memory would take over and again and I would soon forget about it. I never thought about how these events affected Rick. It was getting stressful for him to go places with me.

In May, we went to a retirement party at a private room in a restaurant. It was a fun and easy night for me because everyone was drinking. I had already downed my usual Friday amount at home so now I could have several more glasses of wine and I would look just like everyone else. As I stood up to go to the restroom, I had trouble walking straight. I felt my legs zigzag across the room. When I got in the bathroom stall, it felt good to relax for a minute. The next thing I remember, a fellow teacher was knocking on my stall door. "Kerry, are you in there? We've been worried about you because you've been gone so long." I had "fallen asleep" on the toilet. I vaguely remember my head bobbing around and feeling overcome with sleep. "I've only been gone-uh-minute," I slurred. Apparently I had been gone for fifteen minutes and Rick had sent her in there. *What's the big deal anyway? Do I need a babysitter now?*

I often forgot about important decisions that Rick and I had made together. We had agreed not to get another dog. When I heard about my coworker's yellow lab that was up for adoption, I went to get her. Rick was angry and confused when I came home with Abby, who was a crazy ball of energy. I hadn't even bought food, dishes, or supplies for her. There had been no planning, thinking, or communicating. Rick knew I wasn't capable of caring for any pet. I only wanted what made me tentatively happy. Abby immediately loved Rick, but seemed apathetic about me. She quickly became his dog. The only attention I gave Abby was when I was drunk and played with her. I ran around the house and chased her to take her toy away. I fell down often and sometimes didn't get up for a while. The kids, who were young adults now, came home and saw me chasing Abby. I thought they would join in with the game but instead they looked at me sadly. I dismissed the memory of their expressions. *What was their problem anyway?*

My trip to the eye doctor is another event that should have been a warning to me that I was losing control. I had needed eye glasses for a long time but could not get used to wearing them. Part of the reason I couldn't wear glasses, I am sure, is that my vision was blurred from drinking. I decided to try and wear contact lenses. In order to get used to wearing them, I had to follow the daily prescribed gradual increase in time. I would come home and put the lenses into my eyes for several hours in order to get used to them.

One night, I couldn't get a contact out of my eye. It had disappeared far up under the eyelid in my attempt to reach it. The lens was impossible to reach. After a half-hour of poking, swearing, and eye-washing, I gave up. I went and called the optometrist. Thankfully, they were still at the office and agreed to wait for me to get there. "You're NOT driving yourself," Rick intervened. This time, I was thankful to have his help. As I got into the examining chair, I remembered the obvious things that anyone, but especially a doctor, would easily notice; my breath smelled of alcohol, my pupils were dilated, and I could hear my own inebriated speech. In an effort to cover up, I said "I probly smell like wine. I usully haf-u-glass after work." He was kind and said very little. "You should take a few days off from trying to wear the lenses. Your eye is pretty irritated." was his only response. I thanked him for seeing me but felt the embarrassment even through the buzz of alcohol. Once again, I dismissed the nagging regret of my own consequences.

There were many drunken episodes that should have convinced me that I was in trouble. I was behaving irrationally when I yelled at the dairy case because the store was out of my favorite yogurt. I also yelled at the self-check scanner, and finally, at the clerk. Sometimes my actions were even delinquent, such as when I refilled my own alcohol container with soda at the movie theater. Risk taking and moral decline were gradually taking over. Driving under the influence is something that still troubles me. I would never have believed that I was capable of these kinds of behavior. How can a person go that far from her own *self*?

I recently heard a song on the radio that describes how I became this entirely different person. The words to *Slow Fade* by Casting Crowns say it well;

It's a slow fade when you give yourself away
It's a slow fade when black and white are turned to gray
And thoughts invade, choices are made, a price will be paid
When you give yourself away
People never crumble in a day
It's a slow fade, it's a slow fade

It's so true. I never saw the sneakiness of the demon. I never felt the insidious slide. I never heard the gentle warnings. It was one small, compromising step at a time.

## *Rick's Reflection*

### I Was Clueless

Looking back, I'm quite amazed at how dense I was. Sure, there was the occasional wedding or family reunion where she overdid it. I recall thinking that she just couldn't hold her alcohol. I barely saw her finishing more than two or three drinks. And though I'd join her, I always had to pace and limit myself because I was the designated driver. In fact, she would harp on that. She would lecture me, and later the kids, on how easy it was to blow a DUI. *It only takes two beers to be legally drunk*, was her favorite mantra. I later realized I was being set up. She couldn't relax and let loose if she didn't have a sober driver.

But looking back, it wasn't all that occasional. Every time alcohol was served in a socially acceptable setting, she over-did it. I was slow to catch on. It was the perfect camouflage. A drunk could hide in plain sight among other drunks. The awareness snuck up on me. How did this happen? When did the normal become chaos? All the signs were there, yet I just didn't see it. I remember her once confiding in me how she bought herself a quart of beer while grocery shopping only to down it in the parking lot. She just wanted me to know. She was concerned and wondered if we should cut back.

She was fine. We were fine. But if it makes her feel better, we'll cut back. We'll limit ourselves to weekends. Hell, I'll quit altogether if it's that important to her. I didn't see it, but I was willing to go with it. Drinking was never really all that important to me. I liked it, but if we needed to I could easily give it up. In fact, we did. For several years.

Our local church didn't drink. I don't really recall if it was a requirement or if we just chose not to because no one else drank. But we quit for a good fifteen years. And it was perfectly timed to when we were raising our kids. We could be Godly church leaders and good parents at the same time. It worked. Years later while visiting Kerry in rehab, I noticed a young twenty-something dad unbuckling four small children from his car to visit their mom. It struck me hard at the time how that could easily have been me and what a gift those fifteen years were. A gift from God? A gift from Kerry? I'm not really sure if it matters. But I was sure that of all the bad choices she made in later years, this one she did right. She knew the value of being a mom, and somehow was able to muster the fortitude to give her family the gift of a sober mom, when it most mattered.

But the dry spell ended eventually. It was about the time our oldest had graduated high school and was spending less and less time at home. Kerry suggested it might be okay if we drank on the weekends. Sure, why not? I never had any issue with it. Sobriety had been her idea. I just didn't want to be the irresponsible dad—the bad example. And so, a bottle of wine made it into the grocery cart each Friday. And I remember thinking how nice this was. We'll kick back at the end of a hard week and split a bottle over dinner. Soon we'd have another on Saturday and one bottle became two. Then the weekend was commencing on Thursday and stretching into Sunday night. And before long, wine in the evening became our daily thing. Which was fine—nothing wrong with a glass or two to unwind. After all, Jesus drank wine. Very scriptural, very normal.

But I didn't always have wine. Sometimes I just wasn't in the mood. Yet Kerry never missed a night and often became irritated when I passed. *What, so you're better than me? You're too good to drink on a work night?* Sometimes I'd blow her off as just being in a mood, but usually it became easier to just join her. She was meticulous about splitting the bottle evenly. *How many glasses have you had? Here, have your second glass, I already had mine.* And I couldn't help but notice how she could get lit on the same two and a half glasses that I had. And again, she'd push me to regulate her. Not a problem. We'll just cut back.

She would always initiate the concern. *We just can't be drinking this much. Why are you buying so much wine? I thought we were going to stick to just weekends? You can't let me drink this much?* And I began to puzzle on how this became my fault? But if I tried to suggest that we just take a break, that was suddenly crazy talk. *I'm not saying quit, just don't buy so damn much wine. It's not good for me.* And you would think that this would've given me my first clue. But instead I just accepted that as husband I was responsible for setting and monitoring limits. Okay, I can do that. I'll try to set limits. That's my job—to set limits. And the cycle continued.

# CHAPTER
# 7

## WORK WAS BECOMING
## UNMANAGEABLE

For several more years, I still believed that I was living with a solution for life's struggles and problems. When I did feel stress, drinking would always enable me to escape the feelings. When I got up in the morning, it was increasingly difficult to get myself on track. As time went on, I became completely physically addicted. My blood pressure began to rise and I would begin to shake if I didn't get to my drinking by four o'clock. People still didn't know about my drinking. I was living the perfect lie.

Work was becoming unmanageable. I was having shaking episodes during the day. One day, my principal came into my classroom and asked for my signature on a document. I panicked because I knew that I couldn't write my name legibly that morning. When she gave me the pen, I paused and drew her attention to a student. As Mrs. Brown went to the student, I breathed a sigh of relief. While carefully placing two hands around the pen with my fists resting on the table, I slowly and carefully was able to make my signature look close to normal. Thankfully, Mrs. Brown did not see me do this. One of my kindergarteners said, "Why are you holding your pen so tight, Mrs. Sam? What's wrong?" I never answered.

Co-workers noticed my tremors. They asked me if I was alright. I told them that I was having blood-sugar issues. They seemed satisfied with this explanation.

When I wasn't at work, I was drunk. I had no friends anymore. We were still attending church but I hadn't connected socially because I didn't attend anything. I just drank. Our church was just big enough that people didn't notice your absence. Old friends gave up calling me. I would decline getting together because they didn't drink and I couldn't stand not to. I found out later, I would occasionally call an old friend when I was in a black out. The conversation was completely one sided as I went on and on, running my words together. Sometimes I would remember dialing the number but couldn't recall anything else after that. People were finding out about my secret. I was just unaware. In my times of sobriety, I chose not to think about these events.

I still prayed. As a matter of fact, I cried out to God every morning. I asked Him to get me through the present physical sickness and to help me stop drinking. I told Him I would stop. At that moment, I sincerely wanted to stop. A number of times, I poured out what alcohol was left in my attempt to make a clean start. But every day, I would be drunk by four thirty.

In my efforts to quit drinking, I would sometimes leave myself no alcohol for the following day. If there was nothing for me to drink when I got home, I thought this would enable me to quit. On one of those *experimental zero-alcohol days*, I felt heavy withdrawal, and I panicked. As soon as my students were on their buses and heading for home, I got in my car and drove to the back door of the liquor store. I didn't like to buy alcohol in our small town because everyone knew me and *my story*. I practically ran out of the door after buying my bottle. I poured it in my travel mug and downed it. As I returned to the building to gather some work, I remembered that there was a staff meeting. *Damn!* And I was late for the meeting now. I didn't care because my addiction had been fed. I was calm and in control as I entered the meeting room. I sat as far away from others as possible and tried not to engage in conversation. My speech already felt rubbery because I drank so fast on an empty stomach. It seemed to me that no one was noticing any of my symptoms. I believed that I had successfully beaten the system. I believed I was a successful and functioning alcoholic.

As I drove home that day, I lost control of the steering wheel of my car. I went off the road and into a yard. I made a donut like shape with my tire marks in the grass. Feeling shaken but confident from the high, I got out and decided to do the right thing and own up to my mistake. *After all, I'm an honest person.* I couldn't just drive away. I rehearsed what I would say; *"A rabbit ran across the road in front of my car and I swerved to miss it."* I knocked on the door of the house several times. *Good. Now I won't have to lie.* When no one answered, I got back in my car and found my way onto the road, all the while grateful that no one would know.

One day, the superintendent was making rounds and visiting the classrooms, which he periodically did. I froze when I saw Him. He must have seen my shock. *Does he know how hung over I am? Just act normal. What is normal?* I had been demonstrating to my kindergarteners what to do in a fire drill, because we were about to have our first practice for the year. I was using toy animals to show the students why it was so important to go through the doors in a line as opposed to a mob. While I was in the middle of this, a student started screaming from the bathroom. I quickly got up to go see what the problem was. I almost fell over because I was unstable from the morning withdrawal. Did Mr. Mann see that? After helping the student out and calming him, I was shaking uncontrollably. I took a deep breath and tried to get calm. When I approached the group area, Mr. Mann was tying a child's shoe lace and calmly talking about recess. He looked up with a neutral expression. My constant paranoia kicked in. *I think he does know! Is he trying to look normal for the sake of the kids?*

Another day, I was working in my classroom after school. After returning with a bottle, I passed out with my head on the table. I woke up several hours later with the room almost dark. Had anyone seen me? Did a colleague come in to talk with me, or worse yet, a parent? When I got home it was past dinner time. I hadn't even planned anything to cook. *I will just drink tonight.*

At the beginning of Christmas break, the administration team went out to dinner. There was a group of about sixteen people meeting at a restaurant. Since I was becoming a recluse, this created a dilemma for Rick. I felt increasingly uncomfortable with socializing—especially with groups of people. And these were *important people.*

As I was getting ready for the evening, I was trying to plan my drinking. Of course the administrators would be drinking since this was a holiday celebration that took place after work hours. *Could I drink my normal amount with all of them?* I would look silly ordering eight glasses of wine. During a few hours I would normally drink three tumblers full. That would not be appropriate in the restaurant, even though they would probably drink. I could picture it now; they would share a bottle of expensive wine between about four people or they would order by the glass and have one or maybe two glasses. Some of them wouldn't even finish their glass and would actually leave it there to be discarded! In the past, I had guzzled down the glasses of wine that were left behind at parties. It was unbelievable to me that people left perfectly good wine in their glass.

That evening, I decided that I had to begin drinking early so that I could look like *the normal drinkers* at dinner. I could order just two glasses of wine at the restaurant if I had already downed several tumblers full beforehand. That would calm my nerves and give me the confidence I needed to socialize freely. As I was getting ready, I began to drink my usual amount. When it was time to leave, I needed more alcohol to face the stressful evening. My nerves were worse instead of calm so I poured a travel mug of wine to take with me. Rick and I had always taken water with us in the car so it did not occur to him that I might have something else in the mug. Apparently he smelled the alcohol. As we pulled into the restaurant parking lot, Rick asked, "Do you actually have wine in that mug?" *Of course, dummy,* I thought to myself.

By the time we got to dinner, I was feeling pretty loopy. I was pleased to meet the superintendent's new fiancée, Janis. New people were always easier to sit with because I could just keep asking all about them, with little focus on myself. As I pulled out the chair next to Janis, Rick said, "Ah, Kerry, I think the Allmans were already going to sit there." I sat down anyway because Janis and I were in deep conversation about her diamond. We talked easily and things were going smoothly. Rick leaned over and asked me not to order any more to drink. *Yeah, right.*

In an effort to be agreeable, I ordered something unusual from the dinner menu that was suggested by Mr. Mann, the superintendent. When my plate came, the dish had crayfish in it. "Oh, no-o-o!" I yelled. "There are bugs in this! And I believed you, Jack," I laughed artificially. "You got me good!" Mr. Mann looked embarrassed. I ordered more wine and ate very little. Soon I was in a blackout. I opened my eyes and saw the crayfish only inches away from my face. I could no longer hold my head up. It just kept swooping toward the plate. Rick explained that I wasn't feeling well because of some new medication. "Tha's right, med-cation," I slurred.

By this time, the whole table was quiet and uncomfortable. I could sense that even through my drunkenness. We tried to leave but my shoes were lost somewhere under the table. I slid down in my chair and stretched out my feet to try and snatch them. As Rick crawled under the table to retrieve my shoes, I vaguely sensed his humiliation. The strappy dress shoes just would not go on my feet. My legs kept crossing and bending uncontrollably. I began to laugh hysterically. "I'll just go barefoot." Rick was attempting to hold me up while still clutching the shoes. "Ya don' need to hang on ta me!" I snapped. "Just don't talk anymore!" he whisper-yelled. I don't remember anything about going home that night.

The next morning, I felt so relieved that Rick had told them about the medication. I actually had begun to take an antidepressant shortly before this. What a brilliant excuse! And no one would have a clue that I was drunk. I believed that they didn't know I was drunk because of what Rick had told them. Everyone knows that you shouldn't mix even one glass of alcohol with certain medications. I kept asking Rick for several days if he thought they knew I had drank too much or if they actually thought it was just medication. I was obsessed with figuring out what they all thought. He got tired of the same questions over and over again and finally yelled at me. "Of course they know. Everybody knows!" This started a huge argument, which was becoming more and more common for us.

Did I even think about Rick's situation? I was manipulative, fearful, and egotistical. He was a new administrator and I was much more than a small embarrassment to him but I couldn't see any perspective but my own. I was now directly jeopardizing his standing. That was the first time Rick had to cover for me and it wouldn't be the last. He was in a tough situation, and at the time, I was too self-absorbed to even notice that I could affect his job.

Some days later, at an administration meeting, my principal asked the group what to do if they believed a staff member had a drinking issue. Rick came home and told me what they had said and that they were aware of my drinking. I didn't believe him or, rather, I chose to look the other way. *They must be talking about Jeanie,* I decided. *She drinks way too much.* I had been pleased to hear that there was another staff member who got crazily drunk at a staff Christmas party. I thought that her incident would overshadow any talk about me. But people at work were recognizing my drunkenness after school each day. They were starting to watch and see if I was under the influence during the day.

Spring break was an endless drunk. We didn't go anywhere that year. I decided to do some painting in the house. There were many paint *accidents*. I tracked paint down the hallway and onto the carpet. I remember painting a ceiling in the middle of the night. Paint was getting in my eyes so I put on Rick's glasses to keep the paint out of my eyes. It never occurred to me that I couldn't see very well. I missed many spots and had to repeat the painting several times. When I got done I looked at the clock. It said two thirty. It seemed like eight thirty. I went to bed and woke up in the dark. Was it morning or night? The clock said six thirty and I didn't know what day it was. *Should I ask Rick? No way. I'll turn on the TV.* I passed out in front of the TV for a long time.

*I know I can't go to work. I'm screwed. I have to drink.* Those were my thoughts as I awoke on the first day back to school after break. There was no way I could get myself sober. *I have to call in sick.* I couldn't get out of bed without my head spinning and exploding.

*I'll ask Rick to call in for me.* Then I wondered if I would be able to get detoxed enough to go back the next day. *God! Please hear me! I'm ready to surrender to your way!* I heard a response. "**Take a medical leave.**" I couldn't believe that was the solution. *What?* I figured I was making up the God voice. That didn't sound like Him, but yet I knew it was. *Please deliver me! I need freedom now!* When I heard nothing more, I decided I would pray again later when my head was clear.

Tuesday morning as I got ready for work, I was still overcome with waves of nausea. I hadn't taken God's advice. Pride and craving won again. I was going to look normal. Normal people didn't take medical leave for drinking.

On that Tuesday morning, I considered what it would be like to drink in the morning. I knew that it would make me feel better. The shaking and withdrawal would stop. *If I just took a few sips of wine, I would feel much better.* That would be crossing the line. That would mean I would actually be under the influence while I was with students. *Besides that, I will smell like wine!* I had grown so accustomed to keeping myself at a constant buzz the previous week that it seemed more normal to be drunk than sober. I wrestled with myself so long that I lost track of time and was borderline late getting to work. I tried to encourage myself; *I managed it! I kept myself from drinking! I still have discipline . . .*

# CHAPTER
## 8

# THE WEDDINGS

After almost twenty-eight years of marriage, both of our daughters became engaged within a few months of each other. This was a joyous and busy time, but not without the stress of planning and preparation. I was very happy for my daughters because I felt that both had found amazing husbands. It seemed that our years of praying for the future spouses of our children had been genuinely answered.

The planning of the weddings and receptions was something I had always looked forward to. Though I was drinking nightly, I managed to help with the preparations and be supportive. I helped with the necessary arrangements but I am not sure now that I was sensitive to the desires or needs of either of my daughters. I gave opinions often and sometimes forcefully. I did not heed the advice that was given by the groom's family nor did I care about their input. When gently asked about a decoration, I flatly stated that part of the lace was from my own wedding gown trim, and it wasn't going to be changed. I had assumed that my future in-laws were being critical. *My daughter was okay with it so why were they concerned?* These thoughts and attitudes were mean and uncaring. I had never behaved rudely before to newly formed acquaintances; especially to people with whom I would later want to maintain good relationships. I was vaguely aware of these costly changes, but unable to keep myself in check. These are regrets for which I have since had to make amends. I was starting to destroy relationships and sabotage events of people I loved the most. However, I still firmly believed that I could drink alcoholically while maintaining success in all parts of my life.

At my prodding, the wedding invitations followed the same template that I had used for my own wedding. I was not open to other suggestions from family members or my daughters. However, the wedding invitations would never have successfully gone out in the mail if I had been in charge of that. When gathering contact information for the invitations, I could not read my own handwriting. That meant that some addresses were either incorrect or missing and we had to go through the process of finding those addresses again. I could not keep a straight count on the response numbers for the receptions. Every time I counted, the number was different.

Because of my excessive, controlling involvement, I decided that I should be the one to make the alterations on Samantha's bridesmaid dress. I procrastinated and did not get to it until midnight the night before the wedding. I kept falling asleep, waking up, drinking, and then sewing a little more. This could easily have been disastrous.

Most importantly, I do not believe that I was emotionally or spiritually sensitive to my daughters during these months of planning. The priority of meeting their needs was overshadowed by my constant guilt of being a drunk. I tried to make up for this lack of intimacy by focusing on the physical part of planning. There were times that I could've prayed with my daughters or asked them if they were nervous or had second thoughts. I ignored that stuff, even when my daughter Kylie seemed emotional. *She'll figure it out. I'll ask her friend Ashlie to talk with her.* Those were my inner responses.

Now I sometimes wonder if I wasn't reliving my own engagement time because I had always desired to redo my wedding plans. I had been so young and hurried when I planned my own wedding, that I quickly chose things that I disliked later.

Another thing that I can now see clearly about that year of the weddings is my lack of close relationships. When making guest lists for wedding showers, I was having a difficult time finding people with whom I had maintained contact. During the previous years of drinking, I had not returned phone calls or responded to invitations from old or new friends. That left me feeling guilty about inviting individuals to a shower with whom I hadn't spent time or energy fostering the relationship. I hadn't seen a need for friends over the past few years. I couldn't be drunk and spend time with any of my friends. Being left alone to drink had been my final preference.

After the weddings, I insisted on maintaining total control of the photo proofs. Since I had paid for them, the wedding pictures were not allowed to leave my house. There were no options offered or discussed. The girls had to order from the collection that I maintained and I would keep all the original photos. I was clearly behaving in a strangely self-centered and rude manner!

It sounds like I am beating myself up. You might wonder if I am experiencing emotionally dangerous remorse. It is actually helpful for me to rethink my actions without allowing regrets. I never want to repeat this kind of destruction to myself or those I love. I cannot have do-overs or makeups but I can *stay fixed.*

So what happened at the weddings? Did I pull off good behavior? I was carefully and dramatically warned a number of times by Rick to refrain from drinking on the day of the wedding. *That was ridiculous! Zero amount of alcohol brought out the violent and crazy behaviors.* It would be worse than drunkenness. *Didn't he get that by now?* Though I was angry about his interjections, I knew Rick was right. I could NOT ruin their special day. I had a strong hunch that Kylie and Samantha had asked Rick to talk with me. For once, I gave in to reason. I would not ruin their day, but I would drink.

I very carefully planned each step of the wedding day. Drinking plenty of water and actually eating food, for once, were part of my plan for the day. *See? I know how to drink right!* I waited as long as I could to start drinking while I was getting ready. I really wanted to down several tumblers because this was a big emotional event. That is what I always did on social occasions. The more social the event, the greater the amount of alcohol it would take to get through it. *How could I possibly be expected to stay sober for four hours before the reception?* Even then, I couldn't be racing up to the bar every ten minutes when I arrived. In my carefully thought-out plans, I had purchased some eight-ounce bottles of wine earlier that week. I placed three in the glove box so I could switch them out later, and three in my purse, wrapped in paper towel so they wouldn't clank together. I downed them in the bathroom stall at the church and then again at the reception. One bottle at a time was just right. I felt relieved and yet I could still walk straight. I maintained appearances and drank several glasses of wine like the normal people. I was later told that I was presentable and that, unless you knew my circumstances, a person wouldn't have guessed my amount of consumption because I fit in with *normal wedding behavior*. There were only a few questionable moments that I remember. First, I sang loudly into the microphone at Samantha's reception as part of *Love Song Karaoke*. Secondly, I forgot names and etiquette when making some of the introductions. *"I think you are Uncle Bill? This is Samantha's Grandpa."* Finally, I coerced a group of coworkers into singing a kindergarten friendship song with me as part of Kylie's reception entertainment. But these were the behaviors of a *normal drinker* at a wedding. These were the behaviors of a nervous mother of the bride. These were the behaviors that upheld my denial.

I know that my daughters were praying for me because for the first time ever I embraced the idea that I had to maintain at least partial sobriety. It was their day. It had to be about them. My only wish now is that I could've been more focused on my daughters than on myself and my drinking.

Miraculously, the wedding services and receptions were beautiful and memorable events. The pictures were even a success!

There it was again. The fuel that told me I was going to be okay. Even though I was an alcoholic, I could be in control at every event—even highly important ones—and people would not find out. I had maintained normalcy and I had upheld expectations. I was a successful, functioning alcoholic and I felt emboldened.

# CHAPTER
# 9

# FIRST TREATMENT

Rick was getting worried. He began to talk to me about my consumption, although he still had no idea how much I was actually drinking because I hid the boxes of wine. I hid them in the garage with my garden supplies. I hid them in my clothing storage boxes. I hid one in the bathroom cabinet behind the cleaning supplies. Rick thought he was keeping track because I would let him retrieve two or three boxes at a time under the bed. I would sneak the extras into the garbage. He was drinking a small glass a day like normal people do. In reality, I was drinking at least five.

He knew that my luck was going to run out and that there could be serious consequences. People would find out soon. I never denied my problem. I knew I was an alcoholic. I simply thought I could beat it. I really believed that I could continue to live my life while maintaining alcohol addiction without receiving any consequences.

Finally, because Rick continued to badger me and because it was summer, I agreed to go to treatment. *Actually, maybe this would look good.* It would seem like I was trying to get better. Maybe I could get better. I finally agreed to go to treatment under one condition; I wanted to go on a vacation first so that I could enjoy part of my summer. *Let's face it. There will be no more summer fun once I go to treatment.*

The vacation was unforgettable. We went to the Upper Peninsula. We had no real plan so we just roamed around, staying wherever we landed. We slept and ate whatever and whenever we wanted. We hiked and took a boat cruise. I even had a *Bloody Mary* for breakfast. It was July so Rick joined me in my drinking, except that he was still responsible and knew when to quit. He noticed that I was oblivious to rules and norms. I used to be so caught up in the opinions of others that I would squelch spontaneous fun because it might draw even the smallest amount of attention to us. He decided to join me in my fun-loving behaviors. He had always been a believer of trying something new while on vacation. Our hotel had no pool. I desperately wanted a pool one night. I suggested that we go in a back door of a fancy hotel to use their pool. When someone went out, we entered. Because I was drunk, I was confident enough to walk in like I belonged there. Thankfully, we were not noticed. I laughed uncontrollably the whole time we were in the pool. It was partly fun just because we never did anything like that. Another evening, we were hanging around a pool where we were staying and I befriended some bikers. I invited them to see our room and they showed us theirs so we could compare the thematic décor. This made Rick nervous. I had no sense of reality or concern for safety. Another day I jumped off a high pier into Lake Michigan with a group of teenagers. On our way home, I continued my adolescent behavior as I carved our initials into a railing on a scenic platform. This delinquent action still puzzles me. I would never, ever disrespect property—especially state forests. I wasn't even afraid to use the woods or the weeds to take a bathroom break. The one thing I attempted that was completely unacceptable to Rick was that I tried to drive to the party store drunk. Thankfully he intervened and went instead. *Now he finally understands my need for alcohol. Will he continue to go to the store for alcohol when we get home? We'll see.*

Fond memories like this vacation are what make me think about drinking sometimes. I have what is called *euphoric recall.* I only remember the fun times and forget the embarrassing, sad, nauseating, illegal, and even dangerous times. It has been important to realize that as I carefully recall each story, my selfish actions display rash, impulsive thinking like that of an emotionally impaired adult. At the very least, these actions display extreme immaturity. My goal to escape from reality continued to blind me.

Vacation ended, and I was begrudging and fearful about going to treatment. *Why had I agreed to that?* I couldn't detox myself to go to treatment. I was shocked to find that I was completely physically hooked.

After my initial assessment and intake at the rehab unit of St. Andrews, I heard the nurse say, "Let's call Dr. Scott in to get her checked in to detox." *Did they really say Dr. Scott? I think it is Dan Scott who goes to our church!* "Is it Dr. Dan Scott? I think that he does work in this hospital!" I turned to gasp at Rick who was almost out the door. He knew I was going to back out. He saw the panic on my face. So did the nurse. "Is there a problem?" she asked. "I know Dr. Scott personally," I said, still feeling shocked and betrayed. My stomach was already begging for a drink and now it was beyond queasy.

Rick reassured me. "Do you really think Dan will tell anyone? You know Dan is confidential and trustworthy." That was true. I felt defeated though. Someone else would know. Still unwilling, I finally agreed to stay. Rick couldn't get out of there fast enough before I changed my mind.

Treatment was a unifying experience. I found out that other people drank like I did and for the same reason; they couldn't or wouldn't stop. I belonged.

After detoxing, which actually felt wonderful because they gave me narcotics, I was expected to join in with group conversations. There was a man there who had been drinking all his life and had come in with a blood alcohol level of almost 4.0. He could have died! Instead of being scared when I heard this, I thought, *Well, I have a long time to drink. I've only been drinking a few years and my alcohol level is much less than what this guy's is. Drinking won't catch up to me for quite a while.*

Another thing that went well for me at treatment was that I agreed whole heartedly that I was an alcoholic. I could say it easily. "I am an alcoholic." *Totally.* This is step one, I was told. I admitted I had a problem. This looked good to the staff at treatment. Many patients could not yet admit they had a problem. They were blaming their life situations. My honesty made me look good. They had no idea I was deceived into thinking I could stay an active alcoholic forever. And neither did I.

I was released from St. Andrews after three days but I was enrolled in the IOP grogram (Intensive Outpatient Program). I would be commuting four mornings a week in order to attend both group and individual therapy.

The pattern of denial happened again; I compared myself to another, more advanced case. There was a woman in my group that I became friends with. *Now **she** is in **real** trouble*, I decided. Everyone knew about her drinking because she was such a horrible alcoholic. Her husband was going to divorce her and take all his money away. She didn't seem to care though. She never did admit her problem and I often wonder what became of her.

I was expected to attend AA meetings in the evening or after-noon. Proof of these meetings was mandatory so I was given a form with which to collect required signatures. I attended my first AA meeting and enjoyed it. I liked talking about myself. I made sure they understood that I had completed step one. I admitted my defeat. Some of my thoughts at that meeting were; *I have a chance to recover with no consequences. I don't have a DUI. I haven't lost my family or my job. I still have friends. Yes, I am much better off than anyone else I have seen in the rehab program.* If only I would've listened to myself. Those things could happen to me next. I couldn't see any reality about how addicted I had become. Today I know that this kind of thinking is indicative of this disease.

I was asked to come in and take a breathalyzer test one evening. Of course I failed and was asked to leave the IOP program. "You are not serious about your recovery," the therapist said, shaking his head with piercing eyes. For some reason, this made me sad. I had disappointed someone. I had failed at something important and I didn't usually give up easily when things were difficult or required discipline. I also think that some of the sadness was because I had seen the truth about my drinking and decided to avoid it. I would think about that another time. Maybe tomorrow I would be ready.

At the end of July, we had a family reunion with my husband's family at his brother and sister-in-law's house. On that day, as on so many others, I decided I would maintain my drinking. Again! I wouldn't get drunk today, I thought, I will just drink small amounts to stay functioning. I only brought one bottle with me. Soon that was gone. The day had started out nicely. We had lunch and a gift exchange and I was talking and being my usual *fun self* that came from drinking just the right amount. It seemed like everyone liked me well enough. They were laughing with me and no one seemed to have a clue that I had been drinking. *After all, some of them are drinking quite a bit.*

We started to play croquet. We were divided into teams. My stomach began to get anxious. I was feeling my pulse start to rise. I needed more to drink. After my turn, I excused myself from the back yard and said that I was going to the bathroom. I jumped in my car and raced to a store at the highway exit. There was no alcohol there! I went to a bar and grill restaurant next door. Relieved, I walked in and asked for a bottle of wine. They brought it to me and got ready to open it. "Oh no! I don't want to drink it here. I'd like to take it with me unopened."

"We can't do that," the waiter replied with a smirk. "We don't sell bottles to go."

I panicked. "Can't you sell one that's unopened? It's for a party. We ran out." I was frantic. He went and asked his boss and they decided to sell it to me. I didn't care what it cost, which was quadruple the normal price. I ran to the car and pulled out the bottle. *I forgot about the cork! "Crap!"*

I floored the gas pedal and drove back to the reunion at about eighty-five miles an hour on the country road. I grabbed an ice pick and a pen from the kitchen and went in the bathroom to drink. The cork broke into pieces as I stabbed it, drizzling wine on the carpet. At least it was yellow Chardonnay and not red, I thought. I began to guzzle it as best I could. There were floating cork pieces in the wine but I drank most of it down. I went back out to the croquet game, purse and all, trying to look relaxed. "You missed too many turns," Rick stated knowingly. I couldn't look at anyone else. I looked down to avoid their eyes, which all seemed to be on me. That is when I and everyone else saw the open bottle sticking out of my purse.

I continued to drink for the rest of the summer. During the summer, I enjoyed going for walks late at night. Rick would go with me because he knew I would go anyway and he didn't want me out walking by myself drunk. He tried to keep me quiet. I would yell. I would go on the swings at the park and scream like a kid.

When August came, I was not prepared to go back to the work schedule. I had been drinking almost round the clock. I tried not to think about my physical and emotional unpreparedness. I didn't see the losses that were beginning to happen to me. My husband's family had likely recognized my problem with drinking. I could've had an accident the day of the reunion. The doctor who attended our church had found out about my alcoholism when I went to treatment. I refused to see the early warnings and beginning consequences.

I was too busy drinking and getting things ready in the classroom to seriously consider options of stopping or of getting help.

## *Rick's Reflection*

### The Meaning of Love

"What do you mean they kicked you out of therapy?"

"They decided. They took a vote. They said I didn't take it seriously. I'm known as 'the one who drinks'. I don't need them. I can quit if I want to. I just don't want to now."

So I called her therapist. I wanted to know how someone can fail a program designed for failures. And I was told that she wasn't ready. She hadn't reached her bottom. She didn't want sobriety, yet. She hadn't felt enough consequence, yet. She wasn't desperate, yet. Yet.

And I was told I wasn't helping. I was protecting her. I was hiding her keys so that she wouldn't get arrested, so that she would escape a DUI. I was shielding her from getting caught at work, from getting disciplined, from blowing a positive breathalyzer, from getting fired. She hadn't felt the pain of her addiction. And she never would as long as I was still in the picture. In short, she was still drinking, and it was my fault.

"If you want your wife to find recovery, you have to stop. When are you going to realize you've had enough? And when are you going to realize that she'll die drunk as long as you're there to pick her up? Most husbands would've filed for divorce by now. And most times, it's what saves their life."

And that's what struck me. *It's what saves their life.* I tried what I thought was everything. And nothing worked. The last time she checked in to the hospital her blood alcohol was 0.35. *People don't drink like she drinks and live long.* That's what the intake nurse said. That's what her therapist said. I had exhausted all options. I knew she couldn't continue like this and survive. I didn't know what else to do. I didn't know how to save her.

I didn't have a Higher Power. I had God. And I never doubted Him. I never stopped praying. Maybe this was the answer. Maybe I needed to leave her so that she could live. Maybe I'm the problem.

*Is that it, God? Do I need to leave her? Do I need to let her get desperate? Tell me what to do, God?*

And He spoke. Deep within me, but very clearly, just like He did the night I met Him. He spoke.

*Do you love her?*

Do I love her? Of course, I love her. I've always loved her. I've never stopped loving her. Even when she was at her worst. Even when her personality made her someone else. Have you been watching, God? Have you seen all I've put up with? All I've gone through?

*Yes, Lord. Yes, I love her.*

*Then tell her.*

And that was my answer. I love her. And that's all I needed to know. And that's all she needed to know. But why? I mean, seriously, why? What causes someone to love someone else when no one else would? It was God. It wasn't me. God loves her. And this love that I feel—that I know—I have for her is the love that God has for her. I am not capable of loving like this. I am selfish. Trust me, it's true. I can prove it with example after example. And yet here I am, in the midst of absolute chaos, expressing a love that is totally inconsistent with my selfishness.

At our wedding, we read from 1 John 4, which concludes, *We love because He first loved us.* We picked it because we wanted a *love scripture* unique from 1 Corinthians 13. You know the one, *Love is patient, love is kind.* The one that every Christian and non-Christian wedding uses. We picked it because it was different. We even printed it on our invitations. And here I was, thirty years later, and I finally got that scripture. *I loved, because He first loved me.* It all starts with God's love. He loved me perfectly. He loved Kerry perfectly. And because I couldn't do love any other way but selfishly, God didn't *teach* me to love, or even *make* me love. He just loved. And used me to love her. I love BECAUSE He loved. I loved my wife because He was doing it through me. It was perfect, unconditional love being expressed through an imperfect, selfish husband.

That was all that was required. His love. He was the reason, the source of my love. And His love held no expectations, no conditions. So it was time to stop. It was time to let go of all expectations. If she never got sober, if she stayed drunk, if she ended up in jail or died of her addiction, if she lived on to continue to abuse me and embarrass me, none of that would ever change the fact that I loved her. It wasn't a choice. It wasn't an exercise of the will. It was a revelation. It was a recognition of what was. I loved her, and nothing would change that. Because God loved her. And nothing would change that. What we declared on our wedding day was being realized thirty years later.

It was not a decision. It was not my effort to make her feel better or to be nice or to manipulate her or to convince her of something or to convince myself of something. It was a revelation. It was something I was incapable of producing myself. It was a gift from God. A manifestation of what His love really looked like and felt like.

So I told her. And she said nothing. She just stared. And she continued to drink. Months later she commenced her long, long trek to recovery. I didn't say it to change her. I didn't expect it to change her. Nor do I know if it did change her. But it changed me. It defined me. And it gave me a new understanding of my relationship with Kerry, and my relationship with God, and the meaning of His unconditional love.

# CHAPTER
## 10

# OPEN HOUSE

In August, I had fun getting my classroom ready before the students arrived. I maintained a constant alcohol buzz and focused on creating the classroom décor. I had switched over to drinking vodka because it took a lot less to get drunk and it was cheaper. My preferred drunken state was much easier to attain. In the back of my mind were the thoughts; *How will I get sober before the students arrive?*

Finally, it was the afternoon of the back-to-school open house. I was nervous because I knew that I could not drink before the evening began and I also knew that I could no longer choose to be sober that late in the day. It had proven impossible. Parents, kids, staff, administration, and even school board members would be arriving in only a few hours.

I felt like I had two *selves* that day. One self was the responsible, caring teacher who would be happy to meet the new families. The other self was only interested in managing the intense craving for alcohol. It had taken over. Alcohol was my best friend and it was also my constant evil sidekick. It went everywhere with me and it never stopped talking. *Where and when will you get your next bottle and where will you hide it? You should buy the stronger vodka this time.*

I left school in the late afternoon on the day of the open house and went home to change and get ready. It took a while to decide what to wear. I sat on my bed trying to make up my mind. I had to look just right—presentable and professional, but not too dressed up. I knew the real problem wasn't the clothes. As I put on my makeup, my already nauseous stomach began to churn. That feeling could only be remedied with a drink. *Oh, what's one drink, anyway? A few sips will steady me. NO! I can't drink until after the open house . . . but I have to have a little.* My hands shook as I opened the bottle. I didn't use a glass anymore.

I managed to have what I called *a small drink*. Then I put the bottle of vodka in my bag. It would be there after the open house so I could have some when it was over. As I drove back to school, I prayed loudly, "God help, help, help me!" When I entered the building, I was overcome with fear because I was under the influence. It seemed that I was feeling the buzz more than I normally did. People would smell the alcohol. I could not face the evening. I had to escape. Should I go home sick? I went into the bathroom and locked the door. I opened my bag and got out the bottle. I had to get numb. The two lives were screaming at each other. They were colliding. As I got ready to drink, I actually heard a loud voice in my head; "**Don't do this**!" and again, "**Don't** do this. There will be consequences." God had heard my prayer. He was there to help but I was out of time to talk with Him. The open house was starting. I downed a few more long drinks. Then I carefully used my purse-sized mouthwash and took my time using the restroom before heading down the hall. Several staff members were in the hall and I tried to say very little. As I walked to my classroom, the counselor tried to pull me aside. "Kerry, are you okay? Come on in my office . . . Kerry, please come in here!" She grabbed my arm to coax me in but I ducked away. "I'm fine!" *I can do this and the last thing I need is her help.* My legs were starting to feel unsure, but I was determined. When I got to my classroom at the end of the hall, there were already several families entering. *Why are they so early?* I had lost track of time. After that, I only remember a few things. I recall kneeling down to greet several of the students who wanted a hug or to talk with me. Several parent hands were extended toward me. Because I couldn't continue to stand, I sat on a table for a while. It became an overwhelming sea of faces and voices.

Suddenly, a face came in close to mine; inches away. It was my principal, Mary. "Kerry, we are going to get you out of here. I called Rick, and he's going to pull the car around to the back door." Was this really happening? *Does she know?* My incoherent response was, "WHY? I must 'a had too much med-catin." I don't think she even answered me. *Does anyone else know?* Then I was being escorted out of the room by Rick and Mary. I saw the Mr. Mann, the superintendent standing by, watching. *He's here too?* I slurred a hello. Then I was in the car and the disbelief hit me. It had happened! Now everyone would know! I didn't care but I deeply cared all at the same time. Reality had entered my drinking world and I couldn't contain it.

My thoughts now continued to waver between the real and the unreal. I actually still thought I was going to get up for work the next day and begin the school year like always. *I will go and talk with Mary first thing in the morning and explain the medication thing.* Right! I was still trying out that story! There was an overwhelming obsession about how many people had realized my true condition. I even thought maybe the parents hadn't all noticed. After all, they were busy socializing and helping their children meet classroom friends. How could I forget how fast news travels via word of mouth in our small district?

A certified letter was delivered to me later that night. The superintendent had put me on medical leave until proof of my sobriety and recovery could be given. My classroom would be taught by a sub on the first day of school. *How is a sub ever gonna figure out what to do?* Reality was slapping me again. I downed my bottle. At least now I could drink without worries for tonight.

I would be entering treatment again in order to keep my job. I was trapped and there were no choices left. I did want my job. I knew that without my job, I would have no life. Right now, my job was my only life outside of drinking. If drinking was all I had, I would die.

I chose to try Hilltop Recovery center this time. The patient was required to get on the phone and ask to be put on the admission list. Rick had made the initial call but he was informed that I had to *want* to go to treatment. I had no desire to get sober but I found myself saying "I would like to be admitted for treatment of alcoholism."

"Have you been drinking in the last twenty-four hours?" I was asked. "Yes," I said. "How much have you drank?" The routine questioning felt like I was ordering service for my car. "About a fifth of vodka," I answered flippantly. The amount was more than that because I drank all night after being discovered at the open house. I was starting to feel a little suicidal. I just didn't want any part of my life as it was. It seemed to be quickly shrinking to nothing.

I drank all the way to the Hilltop facility. Rick said nothing because he knew that I wouldn't go if I didn't drink first. Physically, this detox was a hard time. My blood pressure had skyrocketed and I could still feel the intense cravings even through the drugs they gave me to counteract them. I slept with my legs propped up on the wall because I was also having symptoms of restless leg syndrome.

At this facility, there were more people like me who just wanted to drink and didn't want to stop. It seemed like kind of a club. People knew one another from previous stays at this center. "Hey, Buzz-kid! You're on my hall!" I heard someone say to another. I wondered if they had signed up together. Meal time felt more like a dormitory on a weekend than a treatment center. Many patients seemed to enjoy the group sessions and free times socializing while smoking.

A small percentage of people were desperate and ready to find answers. They had received one too many consequences and may have reached the bottom of their drinking. I felt deeply for these patients. For me, too, there were now deep, humiliating consequences. If I couldn't get sobriety, what was going to happen? Now that I was sober, I felt hopeless to even try. I just could not believe what I had done. I would not be the same person again to anyone. I had been respected. Now I would be seen primarily as a drunk. That would be the first thing anyone in our community or school district would think or say about me. "She's a drunk!" Anonymity had disappeared.

I had heard about a therapeutic drug called Antabuse, which prevented patients from drinking by creating the reaction of intense physical illness if any alcohol is present. I don't know why but I found myself asking the doctor about prescribing Antabuse for me. Since I had no will power, I figured maybe this drug would take away the desire to drink by making it miserable and near impossible to do so. I knew that I couldn't stay sober on my own. I still didn't desire sobriety. AA hadn't been helpful at all. I hated AA. That had to change, I was told.

There were AA meetings at the treatment center. People from the surrounding suburbs came and joined us. I noticed that these people were different from those I had met at previous meetings. They were positive and not pushy. I was given a small ray of hope that maybe I could be sober for the long term as they were. I left treatment feeling like I could try it again.

When I got home, I would find a recovery meeting to attend. The last recovery meeting I had attended back home several months previously had been cliquey and negative. I was referred to as "The lady over there who drinks" because I went to the meetings drunk. *Whose fault was that?* I was forced to go to the meetings when I was in out-patient care. Being forced to go took away the incentive for me to get well. It also gave me the feeling of being singled out as a loser. Everyone at the recovery meeting knew that if you had a paper to collect proof of meeting attendance that you were probably in legal trouble. I again looked for something else to blame when I couldn't stop drinking. *They are taking away my incentive to get sober.*

That previous accountability of mandatory AA was only the beginning. Now, after my release from Hilltop, I would also have to gain proof of attending a relapse prevention group and I would be undergoing drug/alcohol testing in order to keep my job. I was given a zero tolerance contract by the school administration when I returned to work. If I ever tested negative, I would be terminated immediately. That was generous and I knew it. It is not possible to teach children and continue to be an active drunk. I think I finally believed that.

There was a tense meeting with the superintendent before I could go back to the classroom. He had been almost a friend before. Now Mr. Mann was aloof, stern and quiet. He read the contract that laid out the terms of my employment. "We have to keep children safe." That was the last thing he spoke to me. Those words stayed with me for a while. *Safe? They had been safe! I had made huge effort to stay free of alcohol during hours with the students!* He was going a little over the top with his show of *policemanship*. As a matter of fact, an officer would perform the drug/alcohol testing. I had never been in any kind of trouble before. This seemed like a bad dream.

My principal thought I should address the staff at our next staff meeting. She said it would be good for them to hear about my absence directly from me. Apparently rumors were flying and they were hearing inaccurate things. *How much worse could they hear?* I made a short statement to the group of teachers. "I went to treatment for alcoholism. Thanks for being so understanding and discreet. You all are the best." Their overall reactions had been very kind and welcoming. I decided to just believe them. I couldn't afford the energy now to try and think about who was talking about me or what they were saying. When voices immediately stilled as I entered the lounge, it was pretty obvious there was talk.

A friend at work asked, "Are you really just going to come back to work? How can you do that? Aren't you totally embarrassed?" Actually, I was numb. There were no feelings so I didn't feel embarrassment. I felt nothing—except regret. I wished I could go back and relive the day of the open house. But would I have done differently? I was pretty sure that I couldn't have behaved any differently nor could I have tried harder.

I completed the school year successfully sober. I didn't feel successful—I felt miserable. But I was sober. The Antabuse was working. I was scared to drink because I would experience extreme illness from mixing the drug with alcohol. I went to AA often and found that I did need to talk and to listen. I also attended a relapse prevention group at the hospital. A substance abuse counselor had placed me in this group under her leadership. It consisted of ten women who desired to stay sober. Those of us in the relapse prevention group became good friends and it was one of the few things I enjoyed that year. It felt like we were staying afloat on debris after our ship sunk. Attendance at this group enabled me to receive the documentation required by the school district for records of recovery.

I couldn't wait for the unbearable year to end.

# CHAPTER
## 11

# JUNE ARRIVED

June finally arrived. I had been planning for it. I had taken myself off the Antabuse in May. Cravings for alcohol had lasted all those months. Freedom from this illness can only come about, I learned, through a spiritual transformation. I hadn't gone that far. I had attended several different recovery groups but I had not totally surrendered because sobriety just didn't seem all that appealing to me. Sober people seemed superficially happy. Rather, I stayed in my own cocoon of resentment and focused on myself.

Maybe the spirituality part of recovery was harder for me because I already had a relationship with God. I had prayed since I was eight, but it seemed like God was silent. Was He ignoring me? He certainly wasn't helping me. I wanted God to just take away the desire for drinking without my having to hurt, to change, or to do any work. I had heard of many people who had received these kinds of instant miracles from addiction. *Were they really an alcoholic in the first place?* I wondered. *Were they hopelessly addicted or did they just like to party?* I had prayed many times and said "God, I am willing to quit now. Please help me get sober." Had I really meant it? Was I looking for an excuse to keep drinking? Was I not listening? I was starting to build up dangerous bitterness about spiritual matters. In the fall

I would try again. In the fall I would be ready for God's help. In the fall, maybe I would get a miracle.

I didn't need to stay sober in the summer. I would go back on the Antabuse in the fall, although I knew I wouldn't because I had already decided I would rather die drinking than be sober. I had spent all those months when I couldn't drink thinking about the choice. I was starting to even have an indifferent attitude about my work. Maybe the indifference came because respect was lost now. Parents and staff no longer looked at me the same. I was a hopeless loser. I didn't know it but I was sinking further into the denial of this addiction.

The second week of June, I stocked up on Vodka and went on a six-day blackout. I never could remember much about this week. I came to while walking by the side of the road. Had I walked to town to get more alcohol? I noticed that I didn't have a bag, a purse, or anything with me.

Suddenly, a child's voice called to me. "Hi, Mrs. Sam!" I looked around and there was one of my students from the past year standing in his yard excitedly waving. I waved back just as I stumbled on the edge of the pavement. "Hi, Billy!" The child's father put his arm around Billy and turned him away from me. They walked toward their house. *Billy's Dad didn't even say hello! Did he notice something about me? Was I slurring? Was I staggering?*

It was then that I heard footsteps behind me. I turned and looked. It was our youngest son, Nolan, who had just graduated. He had been following me. I had mixed feelings of gratitude for his concern and anger that I had a babysitter again. No doubt Rick had asked him to *watch me*. In reality, he probably kept me from going places where I would have gotten into more trouble. Unfortunately for him, Nolan was still living at home for the worst of my drinking.

The next day was Saturday of Father's Day weekend. We went to my parents' home. All my kids would be there. My first grandson had been born in March. I couldn't wait to see him. I planned to stay only slightly buzzed because I didn't want to be totally drunk on Father's Day. I tried to have just a few sips at a time, but as always, it proved to be much more.

We all went for a pontoon boat ride. I couldn't seem to control my conversation. I made fun of my son's girlfriend, which I would never do if I was sober. "Raelynn isn't very pretty is she? She looks like that ugly girl from the Martian movie." After realizing what I had said, I desperately tried to fix it. "I mean, Raelynn has other good qualities, I'm sure . . . I mean, maybe she has a nice personality . . ." I couldn't shut up. The more I said, the worse it got. And even through my drunkenness, I could feel the discomfort.

I got up and tried to make my way to the front of the boat. It was especially hard for me to walk in the already unstable boat. I sat down by my mother. I asked to hold my three-month-old grandson Kevin. Mom handed him over to me and I started to rock him in my arms. My daughter Samantha got up and took Kevin out of my arms. "You're not in a good place right now to hold him," she stated. *What? I was totally fine and now they were judging me based on my history!*

When we got back to the dock, Rick suggested that I go lie down and sleep for a while. This time, I didn't argue with him. I knew that I was about to pass out anyway and I had failed at every attempt to interact with my family. I just needed to get away and think. I slept until we left. When I went to get the bottle out of my bag, it was gone. Someone had taken it. I guessed that it was my dad but I never knew for sure.

As we left, I apologized as I hugged my dad tightly. I had ruined the day for him. It was also his birthday celebration. At the time, I didn't even think about how I also ruined the special day for Rick, my son-in-law, my brother, mother, and all my children too.

On Sunday morning, we went to church. Since I couldn't detox myself, I had to have a drink in the morning or I would be shaking and vomiting from withdrawal. I think the kids thought I would be sober since it was morning and since we were going to church. They weren't usually home to see my drinking patterns and to know how things had progressed. I was drinking round the clock. And that was scary.

As we started singing at church, I must have appeared too happy. I danced and sang loudly. I had to sit down to keep my balance. After the music, I remember talking and laughing about something. To my amazement, the kids got up and walked out, one at a time. At first I thought they were using the restroom. Then I noticed that they were continuing to exit and they were not returning. Rick leaned over and said, "C'mon, we're leaving." I felt abandoned. *How could they just leave us at church?*

A few weeks later, I was fixing dinner on a Friday evening. I had my weekend planned. I had purchased plenty of vodka, groceries, and yard work supplies. I always liked to work while drinking. It helped me feel productive.

A car pulled into the driveway. I saw my son get out, followed by my daughter. *What are they doing here?* They never came home without calling first. I was irritated that they showed up unannounced. *I don't have enough dinner for all of them!* More people were getting out of that one car. My son-in-law and my youngest son were also climbing out of the backseat. "Did you know about this?" I accused Rick angrily. Come to find out, he was also surprised by the visit.

The kids announced that they were not here to visit. They were here to talk about me and about my drinking behaviors. *I think this might be an intervention!* One by one, each child took a turn talking or reading a carefully planned statement. They described their concerns, feelings, and worries about my drinking. *I really need a drink right now to escape,* I thought. How ironic. I was only half listening because I was already pretty drunk. I had little to say when they were finished. They handed me their written conclusions. I think I said that I was sorry they felt that way, but I was not remorseful. I was not even regretful at the time. I was abandoned and misunderstood. I was told that I could have little contact with my new grandson. *They are only pushing me further into drinking because drinking is all I have now.* Those were my accusatory thoughts. I got angrier as the night wore on.

Looking back at that evening is very difficult now. I am both proud and grateful that my kids carried out their heartfelt intervention. I have no doubt now that alcoholism is a disease not only of addiction, but of self-centeredness. I was too stuck on me to take it to heart.

I decided to go back to treatment for the third time. *Maybe I am finally ready.* My kids were not playing along anymore. They remained distant and angry. *They are behaving like they are the parents! They could at least try to understand.*

I returned to St. Andrews treatment facility where I had gone for my first rehab several years earlier. The staff remembered me. One of them just looked at me and shook his head. "You gonna get sober this time? You don't have much time left you know." They didn't give me enough of the drug that eased the withdrawal symptoms. I was pretty sure they did this on purpose to allow me to experience harsh consequences so that maybe it wouldn't seem so easy next time. I decided to leave treatment because they were not helping me detox. I was familiar with the whole wing of the hospital because this is where I had also attended the relapse prevention group from which I was dismissed several weeks ago. I had gone to group therapy under the influence and been asked to leave.

I snuck out of my room and went to another hall where I knew there was a phone. My therapist's office was empty and the door was open. I went in and dialed our home number. Rick answered and I pleaded. "Come and get me. They are being mean! I can't stay here." By this time, a night staff person found me talking on the phone. I was ushered back to my room. I did get more drugs, though, because they realized that I couldn't sleep and would most likely be a problem all night long. In reality, the staff probably didn't realize how much it would take to counteract the amounts of alcohol I was taking in. I was drinking at least one fifth of Vodka each day—usually more.

I managed to stay sober for about six weeks this time. Summer would be coming to an end and I was getting anxious about work.

The church had planned a group camping trip for couples. Since I had completed six weeks of sobriety, Rick assumed I would stay sober for the trip—especially since it was church related.

As we were approaching the campground, Rick noticed that my speech had changed. "Is that alcohol in your travel mug?"

"Of course it is!" I laughed. *He should know by now that I don't go to social events sober.* A few minutes later, a policeman pulled Rick over for speeding. "Do NOT say a word! Not one word," he instructed in his *eighth-grade teacher voice,* as he stopped the car. I was still sober enough to think about the fact that I had open alcohol in the car so for once I listened.

At Rick's request, I only drank a little that night and managed to be *normal* for the evening. We had dinner and a campfire. It was a good time but my thoughts were on my alcohol and what everyone thought. It was always about me and the response of others. *Did anyone know I had been drinking? How will I drink tomorrow?* Stopping was not an option. I decided I would try and keep myself to a minimum. I wanted to drink more, but I made myself go to sleep.

I got up really early. Sweats and shaking were already taking me over. I couldn't go back to sleep so I downed a bottle of orange juice to which I had added vodka. I drove to a store and got some more Vodka. When I returned, it was still early and the campers were not up so I took my vodka and went for a walk. I took a trail by the lake and sat down to rest. It was already hot and I was sweaty so I went for a swim in my clothes. I drank some more and then passed out on the beach, using a log for a pillow. It never occurred to me that I hadn't told anyone that I was going for a walk. When I woke up, I didn't really know where I was so I started down the trail again to look around.

Several hours had passed and I didn't even realize it. Everyone at the campsite was now involved in a search for me. They were worried but Rick was angrier than I had ever seen him. Once he realized that I was okay but totally drunk, he started slamming the tent poles down and told me to wait in the car. One friend tried to get him to stay. Others remained completely silent. They knew Rick was done and they knew we needed to leave. Finally Amy spoke and asked me in a whisper if I felt alright and if I had gone swimming in my clothes. She coaxed me to change before the trip home, which I hadn't even thought about. Rick didn't talk all the way home and I could clearly see his determined hostility. Could we still have friends? *Would these people ever want to go anywhere with us again?* I attempted a conversation. "You didn't have to leave in such a huff. That was rude." He didn't even respond.

What would I do now? No one was left who trusted me in the least. The church friends were the last friends I had left. Did anyone even like me now? There was nothing left to do but drink. Why couldn't I manage the drinking anymore? There had been a time when everything worked out. I had been social and fun. Now all events turned out to be disasters.

Up to this point, when I had prayed for help, I hadn't been totally honest. I thought I wanted help but then as soon as I would get physically ill and the cravings would start, I would forget about my prayer and alcohol became first place again in my priorities. Now I had finally become desperate. It took the loss of my last friendships to produce this in me. These were good friends and I had decided to ruin the trip. Rick might not even stick around. Then what would I do? I couldn't live on my own, especially as a drunk. What about my kids? I think they were about done with me, too. I felt that I was probably irredeemable. I knew that I truly couldn't live a sober life. I was sincerely and finally asking God for help. Even when I was ill and craving, I continued to cry out to God. I would finally give in and go buy alcohol because of the physical suffering but I never stopped wanting sobriety. This was a change. I knew now that God was the only way to get sober. I had exhausted all other options.

## *Rick's Reflection*

### Hope

It was the day before Father's Day. To be honest I don't remember if Kerry had been sober the day before, the week before, or even that morning. It wasn't like there was ever a certainty of what I could I expect. The day usually started okay. Summer days, weekend days, vacation days—nonworking days always had the same progression. She'd wake up sober, talk over coffee about what lay ahead (groceries, church, yard work), and I would convince myself that things could be okay. Even if she drank, maybe she'll maintain control. Maybe it'll be the light, happy, fun kind of drunk. Normal drunk, is what I would call it. I wanted to tell her, *Just know when to stop. Just drink like other people. Just don't embarrass me.*

I always had hope on these mornings. I hoped for normal. The outsider looking in would be baffled. *What is wrong with you? Don't you remember anything? Can't you see the pattern of behavior?* It's not like I was keeping stats, or even paying attention. Everything was measured by the moment. And if the morning was normal, then there was hope that the day would be normal. Logic played no role. Hope was everything. Possibility was everything.

If I was keeping stats, the data would show me that today, of all days, had no hope. Today, the probability of success was as close to zero as it could get. Today we were traveling. Today we were visiting family—her family, her parents. And it was Father's Day, which held high expectation for optimal behavior. In short, I was screwed. And yet, I couldn't see it. Because I was blinded by hope.

We talk about the self-deception, the lies of the alcoholic. *Just one more drink. I'll be fine.* But her lies paled in comparison to mine. My drug was hope; hoping that she wasn't knocked on her ass by her drug. Oddly we were both deceived by the same belief. Hers was, *I can control this.* Mine was, *I can control her.* I was no different than her. We both placed our faith in something that rarely happened.

She never traveled without her tumbler, which we both pretended was filled with tea. The tumbler had a tight top and fit snugly in her big purse which she clutched tightly. If she didn't act silly on the drive over, she slept. Still, none of this was necessarily outside the norm. And it still could be okay. Maybe it would be okay.

And even when she would stumble and laugh at herself; even when she'd semi-doze into her dinner plate, even when she'd make an embarrassing comment, followed by four, five, six more embarrassing comments trying to cover for the first embarrassing comment, even when she'd disappear to nap. I would try to cover and hope. Still hope. Always hope.

Until it reached the point where I could no longer pretend; the point where I could no longer deny the obvious. The trick then became: how do we exit gracefully? How do I get her to leave without causing a scene? How do I gain her compliance, slip out, and minimize the damage? Even among the whispers, the glances back and forth, and the pull asides from Kerry's Mom warning me that "Kerry might be drinking again," I still had hope. Hope that we could find her shoes, get her in the car without a rant or argument or a humiliating attempt on her part to explain her condition. Hope she'd be passed out before we got home so she wouldn't insist on shopping on the way home. Hope that I could get her into bed without physical resistance. Hope that she wouldn't detox too soon and need more. Hope that there was still something left in the tumbler, or in the big purse to get her though the night. Hope she'd stay passed out until morning. Hope she'd color her memory with the myth that she didn't behave "that bad," or better, that she'd black it all out. And that she'd wake up sober; we'd talk over coffee about the day's events, and again hope for normal.

# CHAPTER
## 12

# TREATMENT AGAIN

It was August too soon. I was preparing to start a new school year, and despite growing desperation, I was drinking for the entire twenty-four hours. I had to keep the alcohol level consistent enough to function. Tremors and nausea would take over if I didn't maintain. My thinking wasn't matching reality. I was blaming God for all the humiliations I had endured. He hadn't bailed me out. Yet I had this false perspective of being confidently in control. I felt entitled to drink because I had this terrible disease and no one seemed to have answers.

I had been referred to a new substance abuse counselor. Previously, I had been in two different group therapy sessions. This time, I was seeing a highly recommended psychologist privately. Her goal, I believe, was to get me to see that I wouldn't be able to continue to live in this condition. My life would change. There would likely be medical, social, or legal consequences soon if I didn't change course. The counselor recommended that I give up my job and take a year off to focus on recovery. *What? And have everyone know about my alcoholism?* My mind was still fixated on the thinking of others. I doubt that there was anyone in the whole town who hadn't heard about the drunken open house event from the previous year, but I was still trying to believe otherwise.

Another school year was beginning. It wasn't unusual to spend long hours, even into the night, getting the classroom and materials ready. On one of those late evenings, a colleague found me passed out at my desk. When I was confronted the next morning, I realized I would be questioned, and likely even tested. I called a sub, bolted for the door, and took leave again. By the time I reached my car, I truly was sick with a nervous stomach. Treatment was the only option again. Failure to drink successfully was wearing me down.

I don't remember much about arriving at Hilltop Recovery Facility this time. I do remember that I was shocked to hear that my blood alcohol level was too high to be admitted. I had to go to the emergency room first and get started on detox under medical supervision. It seemed like I spent hours in the ER on a narrow stretcher-type bed. I was too agitated to rest so I got up and went out on the lawn and passed out there. Someone found me and I heard a staff member being reprimanded because I managed to walk out the door without being seen.

The hospital staff called Rick who was just getting back home and said that they couldn't keep me because I wasn't cooperating. He refused to come back and get me. I found out later that he told them that they would have to transfer me to the treatment facility as planned.

I was worn down from being found out again and from the inability to appear in control. I was a failure. A sub would again be teaching my class because I couldn't function. It was a depressing week in treatment. They asked me if I was suicidal. I said no, but alcohol would kill me soon enough. That much I was starting to realize after hearing my blood alcohol level.

When I had gone to the doctor in July, she told me that I was jaundiced and that my liver enzymes were elevated. Those facts came back to me now as I was in treatment for the fourth time. I was not going to make any promises to anyone about getting sober. I hated sobriety and I didn't know how long it would last again this time.

There was a patient in this facility that had already been there six times. He was charismatic and entertaining. Before the lead therapist would enter the room, Ron would stand and imitate her. He over-emphasized her Southern drawl and her charm. Ron would ask questions that would be received with both laughter and empathy. He stood and took a bow regularly. His demeanor enabled the rest of us to feel accepted as a drunk and full of false hope that we could maintain the charade. This man enabled those of us in the treatment center to desire continued denial of our true state. Ron would prompt open discussion about failure at sobriety and the funny, related consequences. He appeared to have a lifestyle of attention seeking and, most importantly, he was successful as a functioning alcoholic.

I talk about this man now because I can see the danger of a careless and complacent attitude toward a lifestyle of sobriety. As alcoholics, we latch on to any hope of continued drinking. The impossibility of obtaining sobriety seemed even more likely as I listened to him. Until an alcoholic has lost all hope of drinking as the answer, there is little hope for getting well. But I had gone farther down the slope than him so I knew he was wrong. Even though I wanted to live as he was, I knew that I was beyond it. He had a job that allowed and even provided him repeated treatments. Some patients, however, were accepting of his deceptive viewpoint at a fragile time of possible recovery.

In retrospect, I see these things clearly. I later was relieved to learn that Ron was refused treatment again at that facility. He was told to go to recovery meetings and work on his own program. Ron had acquired all the necessary knowledge about recovery that the treatment center could give him. He had chosen not to follow the directives or the suggestions. Recovery requires true sincerity. Maybe by experiencing Ron's attitude, I was able to see my own dishonest reality.

I tried to pray again while I was sober. I didn't feel loved by God because I hated myself. I knew that God was listening and I knew He forgave me but I felt as though my actions would make God regret He had brought redemption. How self-centered is that? I could make God change his mind? I was one of those that create mistrust and hatred for Christianity. I was definitely one of the hypocrites in the church that are often cited as a reason to stay away. This brought increasing self-condemnation.

Somehow I mustered the strength to go back to work. Was I too self-absorbed to see how my actions affected others? Was I too stubborn to acknowledge the shame? Or deep down, I wonder, did I secretly like the attention? Was I looking for a way to be unique? Did I just not care? I ask all of those questions now because I still don't have the answers.

Mental illness does not allow accurate perception. The ability to maintain my job was the permission that allowed me to continue to drink. Even when newly sober, the effects of the craving were still my motive for everything. *Will I ever be able to drink again? Maybe it will work after I give it a rest for a while.*

I was under watchful eyes. That made it all the harder. I underwent drug and alcohol testing. I went to AA almost every day in a nearby town so that I could stay anonymous in my hometown—even though I had long ago lost all anonymity. There was a grandmother of one of my students who tried to encourage me. She was also an alcoholic who had been sober for a while. She would hug me every time I saw her and tell me that I could do this. It was encouraging and I didn't feel like I had received much of that anywhere. There was also a small, loving group of AA people in my home town who remained hopeful for my recovery. That was good for me and it was surprising to still have people believe in me.

I managed to keep free of alcohol through the fall. At Christmas break, I was still craving intensely while attending daily recovery meetings. I wanted to stay sober for Christmas. I knew that my kids might not even come home if I was drinking. Or they would leave if I started drinking. Part of me didn't care. I just wanted the *old life* back. I wanted the life where I could secretly drink—the life I had before anyone knew that I was an alcoholic.

I really hated Christmas that year. If I went anywhere, I felt paranoid. *Everyone thought I was drinking so I might as well do it.* I didn't feel happy. I just wanted to cry. If this is how living feels, then I don't want to live, I decided.

I had agreed to go to group therapy with a substitute counselor over the holidays while my primary counselor was away. There was a small group of us attending. The substitute was a psychiatrist who had lived through major addiction himself. He had lost everything including his work, his marriage, and his family. Dr. Gibbs had spent years recovering and regaining his practice. He had been as hopeless as me. His story and his words were piercing with truth. I knew that he had experienced everything I was feeling. He finally looked right at me and said "You will die if you continue to drink. You need to go to a long-term treatment facility. That is your only chance." His honest diagnosis brought a new kind of reality to me. I suddenly knew that I didn't want to die. Up to that point, I had thought death would be okay because sobriety was too hard and too depressing. "How long is long-term treatment?" I conceded. "At least six months but you will need a year," he said with a direct stare. In my heart I knew that he was right. Something in my perspective shifted that day.

The next consequence could be death. There was nothing that this disease hadn't touched. It had ravaged every part of my life except my actual life. And what kind of life did I now have?

Between Christmas and New Year's, I agreed to go and visit a long-term facility that Dr. Gibbs had recommended. It was a rural facility with about forty residents. The visit did not give me much hope. We toured during patient free time. People were looking defeated and sad. They were too despondent and tired to get up and move around. The atmosphere was very different from the other treatment centers I had been to. There was an air of resignation. People here were beyond caring what others thought. There seemed to be little or no conversation or socialization. A large group was out in the back smoking. I asked a teenager what she thought of the place. "It sucks" was her response. *Was this better than death?* Could I even consider this? But deep down I knew that this was the kind of place that would get me well. It would be painful. The questions again were the same; did I want to be well? Did I want to pay this price? I decided to try one more time.

# Rick's Reflection

## Fix It!

Samantha called. She was my oldest. She wanted to know what could be done for her mother. Kerry's Mom wanted to know what could be done. Her boss wanted to know what could be done. Doesn't she know that there are consequences to her behavior? What was the fix? What solution did I have? Tell her she's drinking too much. Tell her to go back to rehab. Tell her she's hurting herself. Tell her she's hurting others. Make her listen. Make her stop.

Years before, a parent came into my building to pick up her child. She stumbled through the door. Her breath reeked of alcohol. I informed her, "Ma'am, you're drunk. Your daughter is not getting into a car with you." She was furious and yelled she would call the police. I replied, "Allow me" and grabbed the phone. She stormed out. When her husband later arrived to pick up their child, I saw the hopelessness, the frustration, the embarrassment on his face. And yet, as he left, I commented to my secretary, "How could he let this go on? Why doesn't he do something?" Like those who didn't get me, I didn't get him.

My daughter wanted to do something. And she was looking to me to tell her what that was. She was not accusatory, but sympathetic. Unlike others who asked me this same question, she realized it was a tall order. But she still had to call me. Not just because it was about my wife. It was because I was her Dad. This is what I did. My kids could always call me with their toughest problems: bosses, money, kids, marriage—and I would fix it. It was what I did. Or I could at least help them to feel better. I could give them hope. I could give them perspective. I offered experience, wisdom, insight, understanding. I'd been there before and had conquered the issue. I spoke with certainty. Everything was fixable. Everything would be okay.

But this was different, and she knew it. If it was fixable, I would've fixed it by now. Her worry was also my worry. She'd never been here before. And neither had I. It scared her. It scared me more. She had heard something, read something, about interventions. Did

I know anything about them? Was it worth trying? How could I say no? Everything was worth trying. Sure, I'd heard about them. Hell, I even had a book. Read it cover to cover. I hooked her up. She devoured every word. She called and asked questions. We talked, we prayed, she planned. I didn't have the heart to tell her what I really thought. That it was a stupid idea. That it required professionals. That it only worked if you had her bags packed ready for rehab. But she'd been to rehab, been to the ER, been to AA, been to out-patient therapy, was attending relapse prevention, and was seeing a psychiatrist. And yet being browbeaten by her kids was supposed to somehow work?

So when she called and asked if Mom was home, I knew she didn't want to talk. She was launching the plan. "Keep her there. Give us an hour." I said I would. Even though I knew it would piss her off. I mean really piss her off. I knew how it would unfold. *Who in hell were they to lecture me? They know nothing of what I'm going through. They think it's that easy to quit?* Yet what if they were right? What if this is what she needed? Perhaps this was her bottom. Face-to-face with the raw hurt of her kids. Face-to-face with the possibility of losing contact with her grandson. As long as there was a slight chance, I had to let them try. How could I not? I chose not to tell her.

And even though it unfolded exactly as I anticipated, even though it ended badly, even though it thoroughly pissed her off, even though it was an epic failure—they knew they tried. And she knew they tried. She knew they loved her, were scared for her, and were desperate to try anything to save her life. Because—even though we couldn't fix it—we had to try.

# CHAPTER
## 13

# A NIGHT TO FORGET

Christmas and New Year's were over. I had stayed sober. Maybe I could put off long-term treatment after all. It was time to go back to school and I was depressed. It seemed like I hadn't had a break because I was working hard to stay away from drinking. The craving to escape was strong. I couldn't see that I wasn't strong enough physically or emotionally to do a stressful job such as teaching. I thought that because I had remained sober through Christmas, I was competent. That was proof of my wellness. I didn't realize the emotional addiction I had grown to accept as normal. Normal for me was feeling drunk and I just didn't want to feel any other way. I had agreed to go to long-term care but now I no longer wanted to, nor did I believe I really needed it.

I went for a walk down the road to think. I tried to pray and there seemed to be two separate voices talking with me. I heard the encouragement from God; "You can do this. Follow me. I love you and have good things for you. Listen to Dr. Gibbs and go to long-term treatment." I also was plagued with the voice of alcoholism; "You can drink today. No one will know because you're not going to see anyone. You can feel good for today. Work is two whole days away."

I still didn't have the understanding that one drink meant oblivion for possibly the rest of my life. I could easily die drunk. One drink meant that I wouldn't have any control over my actions. I forgot that I would black out and be on automatic drive to stay drunk. There would be no sanity. I forgot the physical difficulty and almost impossibility of detoxing. I couldn't understand that I was extremely ill. I have since learned that both the physical and psychological craving do not leave the body for months. I wasn't recovered just because I hadn't had a drink for three months. Sobriety is complete reprogramming. And you have to want it. I wasn't well enough to want it.

I had proven that I could be sober for a long period of time so now I **deserved** to drink again. After working so hard, I should have some relief before work started again. I also think that I just wanted to drink one more time . . . I drove to the store and bought a fifth of vodka.

When I came to, I was lying on my bed craving another drink. I looked over and was stunned to see the empty bottle. After frantically checking all of my hiding spots, I found no more bottles. *There has to be more. Did Rick take them?* I wondered if I was sober enough to drive to the store. That didn't matter. As always, the desire to drink won out. I would go to the local store even though I hated to be seen in there. Anyone could see me buying large amounts of alcohol. That was more important than the fact that I would be driving drunk. Once again the craving won out. Physically I was panicking.

As I went to gather my purse and keys, I noticed that Rick had also been making plans. He had taken my keys again. Damn him! I yelled obscenities at him but he didn't even respond. He had become numb to my ranting and chose to ignore it this time.

I went to my room and slammed the door. I would show him. I would walk two miles to the store. Getting my coat and boots would be a trick because Rick would notice that I was going out. I found a half full laundry basket and hid my winter clothing amongst the laundry and carried it to my room. Because I knew Rick was watching me, I decided I would have to climb out the bedroom window. He couldn't stop me. "*I'll show him!*"

Even in my stupor, I was a planner. As I layered my socks and long underwear, I thought about camping in the woods that night. I took a blanket, some matches, and a flashlight to put in my backpack. I wanted to make sure that Rick knew not to mess with me again with his constant controlling. He was interfering between me and my alcohol.

I carefully removed the screen, perched on the window ledge, making sure that my feet would be the first to land. Of course I still fell over as I hit the ground, trying not to scream as I landed in the snow. I waded through the snow to get out to the road, avoiding the house lights and driveway. What was normally a pleasant walk seemed to take hours. There were no lights for the first mile and I was pulling my wheeled backpack on the snow covered road which made the trip harder. After I got into town, I stopped to rest by the railroad tracks for a short time. The urgency to drink kept me moving. I finally got to the liquor store and bought two fifths of vodka. I must have started drinking and walking because I do not remember very much for a while after this. I woke up along the dark road lying in the snow near someone's front yard. As I got up and started walking, a car stopped and I heard a man's voice. "You look like you could use a ride." I glanced up and saw an old beater car. "No, thanks. I'm good."

"Are you sure? It looks like you have a ways to go with your bag. Where you headed?"

*Oh crap! Why is he asking twice?* "NO, thanks!" I purposely sounded irritated. *The car isn't moving! Please make him leave, God.*

"Okay. Have it your way," he finally said. He slowly pulled away. Now I became paranoid. *Is he going to come back? He sounded weird. What if he does? Should I cut through the field to get off the road?* I was shaking even with the alcohol buzz.

The local motel was just a short ways up the road. I decided to go see if they had a room there. I just wanted to get inside, away from that car, and somewhere warm besides my home. I needed to be alone to think and to drink. A vehicle pulled up right next to me. I didn't look at the driver. I kept walking and looking down. *OH crap, oh crap . . .*

Suddenly, I heard Rick's voice. He didn't sound mad, but resigned. "Please, get in." I didn't say a word but got in quickly. I was no longer angry but frantic. Then I noticed how upset Rick was. "I was ready to call the police. Do you know how long I've been looking?"

"No!" I yelled.

"But someone in a car was bothering me." We drove home in silence.

I began to plan for long-term treatment. I was resigned to the idea now. I had hoped that I could wait for summertime when it wasn't so obvious that I was taking leave. Rick wanted me to stay home from school entirely after Christmas break because he knew that I would likely still be somewhat under the influence and shaking with tremors but I wanted to get things ready at school and to make sub plans. I was planning to tell Mary, my principal, at the end of the day that I would be taking medical leave for the rest of the school year. When I arrived, however, I had second thoughts. *What if the administration decides that today is a good day to test me? It **is** the day after a holiday break* . . . I suddenly felt ill, grabbed my things, and called a sub. *I guess she will have to figure things out on her own. I can't do this. I am done.*

I drank heavily for the remainder of that day and night. I knew that I wouldn't get to drink again for a long time. We had made arrangements for me to be admitted to Rayland Road long-term facility in three days. On January 5 at midnight, I went to the ER to get help detoxing. I was very drunk and laughing uncontrollably. Since I couldn't sit up in the chairs, I was crawling around on the floor in the waiting area calling out someone's name that I thought was there. "Randy! I think Randy is over there!"

A nurse came and stood over me. She looked up at Rick. "I'm sorry. She can't be on the floor."

"Fine," said Rick. "You try and get her in a chair then." The staff soon found me a bed because I was bothering everyone in the area.

After detoxing, I stayed at Rosewood Treatment Facility near the hospital for several days. I don't think Rick wanted me at home before leaving for long-term care because he knew I was likely to drink again. This was my fifth rehab center and I slept most of the time.

When I wasn't sleeping, I thought about my circumstances. I was resigned to spending at least six months in Rayland Road long-term care. There was nothing else for me to do. I still had some good things in my life that should bring incentive to get well. I still had my husband, my family, my home, and my health. *I should be grateful,* I told myself. However, I was so depressed that I didn't know how I would get any hope. I didn't want to live without alcohol.

It was the weekend and it was also my youngest son's birthday so the kids all came home. They came to visit me at Rosewood, and we were all able to eat a meal together in the cafeteria. I was surprised and embarrassed when I saw them all walk in, but, at the same time, I was grateful to spend time with them before leaving. Nolan was eating his birthday meal with his mother in a treatment center. *Did I even get him a gift?* I couldn't remember if I had already given him one. *How pathetic.* Maybe I could stay sober for Nolan. Maybe my sobriety date could be the same date as his birthday. That would be a true gift.

## *Rick's Reflection*

### Thank God

I remember once being reprimanded by a treatment therapist for my practice of hiding Kerry's keys. I know all about controlling behavior and obsessiveness, and for the most part agree with the Al-Anon model of *Letting Go and Letting God*. But to this day I have no regrets about hiding Kerry's keys. Nor am I delusional about the fact that the strategy was 100 percent effective. I know she drove drunk several times. But somehow by the grace of God, she never got a DUI, and never hurt anyone while behind the wheel. If I helped make that happen in anyway, how can that be a bad thing?

So it goes without saying that her keys were the launch of a great deal of our fights. On this particular day, I was drained and just wanted this all to end. Kerry was supposed to be tapering back but was insisting on going to town for more alcohol and wanted to know where the hell her keys were.

I never got physical with Kerry, even when she got physical with me. But it was late, I was exhausted, I was sick of making liquor runs, and I already had enough vodka hidden away to help her detox so that we could execute tomorrow's plan. And she was sabotaging it. She was ruining everything. I was, at this point, DONE. I picked her up, threw on her bed, told her to go to sleep, and slammed the door. Then I slumped into my chair, hoping for a small break before round two commenced.

I realized I had dosed off when I heard the phone ring. I got up, but it stopped ringing before I could answer. The caller ID indicated the corner gas station a mile up the road. I went to Kerry's bedroom and the window was open and the screen missing. Shit. It's January. Was she dressed warm? Did she wear her coat? Panic and guilt were at the forefront. My first stop was the gas station. Yes, they saw her. She had asked to use the phone, but when she got no answer, she swore and left. The next stop was a no-brainer. Though the gas station reeked of judgment, the liquor store was always a sanctuary of discretion. Whether it was me or Kerry, the MO was the same. We parked on the alley and walked in the back. It got to the point where they would see either of us enter and put the bottle of choice on the counter. No words, no pleasantries, but no judgment. It was all business. Yes, she had been there. I wasn't too far behind her.

Now where? I just drove up and down streets in town. Do I yell her name like a missing dog? Do I make more stops? Friends, businesses, our old pastor? And how long do I continue before I call the police? I can't say for sure how long I drove. I had decided to take all the routes between town and home before I would decide to call. I was heading up the rural road that paralleled the freeway, driving slow enough so I could examine the ditches on both sides of the road. As I rounded the curve, I hit my brights. Someone was walking up ahead. *Please let it be her, God.* As I approached, I slowed, crossed the center line, and lowered my window. I forced myself to be calm. I didn't want to have to chase her down or wrestle her into the car. "Please get in, Kerry." She got in, dragging a bag. As soon as she shut the door, she began to sob uncontrollably. Something about a car trying to pick her up and she didn't know what to do. It's okay. You're safe. It's okay. It's all going to be okay. I promise.

# CHAPTER
## 14

# POWERLESSNESS

As I was packing for the long-term treatment, my thoughts were jumbled. I was purposely moving slowly. We were supposed to be there at 10:00 a.m. It was almost time to leave. "I'll bring you anything that you forget. Don't worry about it. I'll make sure you get your things." Rick was trying to hurry me along.

I was trapped. I still didn't really want to get better and I knew that. In order to gain sobriety, I would need both desire and surrender. I thought I was one of those who would not be able to comprehend recovery. I was sure that I couldn't do it and that I would be found emotionally incapable. And yet, what else was there? My job was pretty much over, unless I received some sort of miraculous pardon. My kids would only interact with strict boundaries. I would not be able to have any relationship with my grandson or future grandchildren. Friends had become nonexistent. I hadn't heard from our church in months. My marriage was reduced to a *patrol and prison system.* My parents certainly didn't get it. They thought I was lacking self-discipline. Now my mother's recent words came back to me. "Your dad quit smoking and I hear that is harder to quit than alcohol."

Self-discipline. Was that really it? I thought about my work ethic; I had gone back to school and achieved both a bachelor's and a master's degree, receiving the highest grades, from the start of my re-admittance at age thirty-five. I had always cooked all our food from scratch. For all three of our consecutive homes, I worked many hours to make the necessary major decorating changes of new paint, wall paper, and window treatments. I had constructed and dug three vegetable gardens by hand. Maintaining a tight budget while successfully caring for our four children had been much more than a challenge. I even used cloth diapers. On several occasions, before the heavy drinking, I had gone on a three day food fast for the purpose of spiritual growth. I had denied myself many things numerous times over the years. It wasn't about my ability to deny myself or to be disciplined. *Was it?*

Was I just insane then? That seemed most likely to me. I decided that was it. I would go to treatment and find out that it was impossible for me to get better. At least I would be making the effort and no one could say I hadn't tried. This would be my sixth treatment facility and Rayland Road was extreme. You had to work hard or get out. They had the highest rate of success of any rehab throughout several states. I had to go and see if I was beyond hope. I was pretty sure that was the case. Beyond hope. What then? Could I go back to drinking for the rest of my life? Would people be content to know that there was no hope and I was just an eternal drunk? Would they leave me alone and let me drink and die? That was how I was thinking the day that I went to Rayland Road.

As we pulled into the driveway and parking lot of the facility, I was overwhelmed with fear. What would these people be like to live with? It felt like incarceration. I had already seen many of them on my visit and I knew that some of them were serving the remainder of their prison sentence here because of drug and alcohol related crimes. "Please take me home," I begged. "I'll do anything else." Rick stood his ground. "Just come for a week. If it's that bad, then you can leave and try something else." We had checked out several other long-term facilities that were more relaxed.

When they found out I was there, the staff didn't waste any time checking me in. They interviewed both Rick and me. As soon as he brought in my prescribed belongings, they said that Rick had to leave immediately. I became hysterical. All the years of dammed up emotions started to come out. We took five minutes in the hall with him holding me and my hysteria continuing. A staff member again repeated that he had to go. I didn't watch him go out the door. I went inside the front office and numbly waited for the staff to give me my next direction. They had assigned me a "sister" who would show me around and get me settled in the bunk area. In the meantime, I talked with Fred, another patient who had just arrived. He saw my emotional state and tried to encourage me. "It's okay. I been here befo. They treat you real good. I won't do no mo drugs, I can tell you that much." I immediately liked him. He was real and he understood.

They brought my belongings into the main room and directed several senior status patients to go through my things to make sure there were no smuggled drugs or alcohol. My *sister* came in, and to my surprise, she was my age. "Hey, welcome! I'm Cindy. I was out taking care of the new bunnies. Wait 'til you see them. I'll take you down the hall when we get clearance. You can't go to your room during the day without special permission." I asked to go to the bathroom. Even that was not allowed yet for me without my *sister*.

I was supposed to remove my makeup, but I had already cried it all off. No makeup could be worn even if you were going off campus with the group to a meeting.

At dinnertime, I saw everyone who was there for the first time. I tried to summarize what I thought about each but it was impossible. The way that I usually categorized people did not work here. You couldn't really tell what was going on with them. Addicts and alcoholics seem to have a skill of creating an emotionless face. I was thankful that they didn't overdo the welcome stuff. Attention or even friendship with these people was not what I wanted. I overheard a guy say "Did you see the new broad? Too old for ya." Laughter followed. There was one young man who seemed different. He never said a word to anyone. He just stared. I felt like he was staring at me.

Shortly after dinner, we were taken to our mandatory, daily local recovery meeting. This was the one time of day that we left the property. We still had to maintain constant contact with our treatment group and could not go off by ourselves. It was crowded at the meeting and we arrived a few minutes late so all of us from Rayland Road sat on the floor. I sat by Fred, my only friend so far. I felt branded with the shame of being a *Roadster*. That was the self-imposed nickname for our group. I couldn't hide behind who I was because now I was just a *Roadster*.

For the first time, I listened to the meeting even though I already knew that I was "powerless over alcohol." That was clear. I couldn't stop crying. Through the shame, defeat, and hopelessness, something felt strangely *right*. Afterward, a kind woman came up to me. She could see my raw emotions. "I'm Mary. Welcome home. Things will get better if you hold on." I sincerely doubted that. I could not imagine life without alcohol.

# CHAPTER
## 15

# RAYLAND ROAD EXPERIENCES

It was a fearful, new experience to sleep in a bunk room with six women who were in the midst of rehabilitation. Thankfully they didn't talk very much to me that first night. The following night the last bunk in the room was filled by a newcomer. As she got into her bunk she said, "Wow. I haven't slept in a real bed with sheets in two years."

"Where have you slept then?" I blurted with amazement.

"I've been sleeping wherever the night job took me, mostly on the streets." I was staring back at her so she continued on with her explanation, noticing that I wasn't following her. "I had to support my habit with prostitution. That was better than living at home." Now I got it and I didn't want to know any more. Unfortunately, I would be hearing a lot more. We would be sharing our past lives at daily sessions.

As I lay there that second night, I didn't sleep for a long time. I was becoming aware that we at Rayland Road had few differences from one another. Our addictions had taken each of us to the same place of oppression and no one was any better off than the person next to them. We had no hierarchy or rank. There was only common loss. We addicts were all grieving that we couldn't have our *drug of choice*. I was no better than Kim, who prostituted herself for drugs. I wasn't a teacher or a homeowner or a church member anymore—or even a mom. We were all hopeless and I couldn't imagine any of us getting better.

A few mornings later, I awoke to a fight in our room. Two women were fighting over cigarettes. One had stolen from the other. "Don't give me that crap! I saw you take one right out of my shirt! May screamed as Bev grabbed her hair. "Pat saw you, too!" May tried to hold Bev against the wall. Thankfully, Pat was able to grab hold of May. "I saw you stealing from Bev the other day. So you f——ing started the whole f——ing thing!" Pat yelled at May. "Now we all gonna be in deep shit if you don't stop!" I had never seen a fight between adult women and I was scared that it might soon involve more of the women. The fear of being heard by a staff member finally won out and they stopped. Bev and May could both go back to prison or possibly end up homeless if the violence became known. Afterward I thought, *Well, that wasn't much different than the fights between kindergarteners. Hair pulling and kicking were the same basic universal reactions. What would I do if someone stole something from me?*

There was one person in the treatment center who was older than me. He was a man of about sixty-five. He had a long white beard and had been living on the streets for a while. Apparently the Rayland Road facility had been charged with trying to rehabilitate Bob. He was shaky and thin. He didn't talk much either. People left him alone for a while but, gradually, the youngest guys saw Bob as a fun challenge. They began to pry and ask him questions. They would slap him on the back and say, "Hey, Bob, did you ever see any action out there on D. Ave?" Bob would smile and give no answer. "Let's go smoke, Bob. You got any smokes?"

When we would pile into the fifteen-person van, which was only for Rayland Road newcomers, the younger guys would leave a space next to Bob. "Hey, Kerry, you sit by Bob. It's your treat!" After a few times of this, I really didn't care. It was better than sitting by the young guys who only talked about stuff like girls, cars, or rock stars. Bob and I began to have conversations about basic parts of our lives. He had been married once, and even had children but had lost all contact with them. I had noticed that the staff did not press Bob to talk at the group sessions so we knew little about him.

The evening supervisor who drove the van would keep tabs on the conversation as much as possible. Many of the staff members had themselves come from a background of addiction. Sometimes, we could get the driver to talk about his or her past. These additional personnel were people that we never saw during the day. I asked one driver how long it took him to be found trustworthy. "I'm not one of you," he said. "I just needed a job and they don't have enough people in recovery to take all these shifts. I like doing this, though. I feel I'm helping to give back." *Wow,* I thought. *We are seen as meaningful community service.* We are the unfortunates of society such as the homeless, the psych ward patients, or jailed inmates. I had never thought of myself that way. Then I realized that yes, our communities were fortunate to have us all off the roads and out of public places; at least until we were *rehabilitated.*

Every morning we had an all-inclusive large group therapy session, or *sharing* time. There were about forty residents. We would pull our chairs into a circle and the lead therapists would join us. This time was often tense and proved to be anxiety provoking for me. The staff would lead the group but we could ask one another questions. We all were required to share on a common subject. Sometimes people were singled out and asked if they were being truthful or if they were taking sobriety seriously. If we didn't have enough support coming from the AA community—visits, rides to meetings, phone calls—then we were asked to explain in front of everyone. I was asked why my plans didn't include a greater **variety** of supporters coming to pick me up. There were only three different women coming to give me rides or take me to recovery events for the next two-week span. A young woman suggested that because I was older, I was probably afraid to ask the younger women for help. I was expected to answer that. I didn't really have an answer. I said that I would consider that and try and find more support. That bugged me a lot. Young people were allowed to give me advice and unwanted opinions about my actions. I guess I still saw myself as more mature and wiser, but I later realized that I had learned some insightful things from those younger than me. The young women were far more socially adept than me. Many could meet strangers with ease and quickly transform a new acquaintance into a friendship.

On Friday afternoon, all *Roadsters* assembled for a weekly update on our progress and status. We were each told, in the hearing of all, whether we had progressed to the next level. If we needed to work on some specific assignments or hadn't met goals, we would stay at the same level until we achieved the number and quality of desired actions. All of these open and constant evaluations in front of the group felt to me like playing dodge ball in gym class. You never knew what was coming next, and sometimes, things felt out of control. I didn't pass to the next level on my second week because I was told that I was too quiet and was keeping to myself, which led to suspicion about my truthfulness and motives of being at Rayland Road. *Damn them! This is how I am! Don't they want me to be me?*

Sunday was family day. I saw Rick's minivan pull in. Oh, good! I was excited to see both my sons, Nolan and Peter. As they piled out, I saw Kylie, and to my surprise, all four of my kids had come, along with Adam, Samantha's husband . . . and Kevin! They had brought my eleven-month-old grandson too! I was so happy to have them all there. We were loud and had fun talking, just like at home. I was happy that my kids didn't seem to feel apprehensive about being at treatment. Most residents were actually near the age of my kids. I felt like I was showing off because I had so many visitors and most residents had so few. It was slightly uncomfortable for that reason. Samantha put Kevin down and he began to toddle around. He had started walking! The whole place was entertained by him. He fell down several times on the living area carpet. Then my compulsive side kicked in. *Kevin might get bad germs here! Who knows what germs might be on this floor!* I picked him up but he wanted freedom. Besides, he didn't really know me all that well. "Let's take Kevin out to see the animals" was my conclusion. *Hopefully, he will remember his grandmother being at rehab or being drunk,* I thought. It had definitely been a day that brought gratitude to my world.

I had learned the schedule and the expectations, and I no longer felt like a newcomer. But there were things that bugged me about some of the rules. I really needed to exercise, and since we could not be alone, I looked for a woman who wanted to walk the trail. I couldn't find anyone. Everyone was either smoking or talking about the couple who just got kicked out for *having relations*. That is how the staff termed it. The Roadsters had their own lingo about the couple. This was a very big deal at Rayland Road because, of course, we were hungry for things to gossip about. Finding the dirt on others got our eyes off of our own shortcomings. Though I was fully capable of joining the talk, I was frustrated that day, because I desperately needed to get exercise. I was rapidly gaining weight. Our time was spent sitting, talking, doing simple chores, or eating.

I was pretty sure that I knew of another couple who was sneaking off to the basement in the middle of the night. I wanted to expose them but I wasn't positive about their actions and I didn't want to falsely accuse them. This could jeopardize their sobriety. I later found out that my suspicions were right and then I wondered if I hindered their recovery by not speaking up.

Daily chore time was a welcome activity for me. I was given a choice between working in the barn or cleaning the main building. I chose to clean the women's bath and shower rooms. I figured that I could be alone in there, and have some time to myself, which I was desperately longing for. Being an introvert, I needed space from people and could never get it here. I also discovered that if I got up early I could have time alone in the commons area. I could read and journal. No one else got up early except Sam, the young guy who constantly *stared.* He wore his iPod and fixed his eyes at the ceiling. That was fine with me because he was looking elsewhere. *What does he think about while staring?* I often wondered. Later I heard that he wasn't supposed to have the iPod so it was taken away. I felt bad for him. *I mean, really, that was all he had and he looked so sad.*

After a month, I was asked if I wanted a different chore. The laundry position had opened up so I decided to work in there, even though I wasn't too excited about touching other peoples' laundry. I was lucky enough to be assigned with another woman almost my age and we became good friends. One day, as we were talking and laughing, some of the young men came in and joined our conversation.

They were supposed to be cleaning the basement recreation area. Someone overheard us and *snitched*. They went and told the staff that we weren't working and that we were all messing around. I was angry. This was the first time I had been able to have a relaxed conversation and someone had lied and ruined it. *What did they think? I was interested in the "youngsters"?* I was moved to kitchen duty, but thankfully, so was my new friend, Leah. When the *Roadsters* found out that we could cook, we received a standing ovation after dinner.

Snitching was a regular part of life at Rayland Road. Sometimes that was necessary, but, at other times, it was just petty or basic misunderstanding. We were actually told to report unusual behavior. *What? We were all unusual!* Just when I thought I knew someone and could predict his or her behavior, something new would surface.

One night, just before lights out, my bunkmate came into the room and said that she had heard the staff talking and that we were going to have a fire drill. "Will we be able to get our coats?" I asked anxiously. "Of course not," she said rolling her eyes. I was not going to go out there in my nightgown—especially in front of all those guys. I frantically began to change back into my clothes. I even ripped the neck of my tee shirt in my hurried frenzy. "Lights out!" we heard. I lay down fully clothed and waited but there was no fire drill. My bunkmate was trying to quiet her laughter with her pillow. Several others were too. I finally joined in. I had been totally duped.

Part of our daily learning involved rethinking our lives. We were asked to write a paper about our growing up years, which we would talk over with our therapist. I was told that the sexual abuse I had suffered as a child was an important predictor of addiction. Drinking was a method of escape. I didn't believe that. I thought I just loved alcohol. I knew that our brains were different and I didn't see how one incident could link to my brain chemistry. *Was this a disease or was it emotional trauma? How could it be both?* I still do not have all the answers to those questions.

One thing that made life at Rayland Road even harder for me and for others was that we were all weaned from medications—unless there was a physical, medical condition. Like most of us, I had been put on an antidepressant several years ago to alleviate the depressive symptoms that were actually alcohol related. Having this antidepressant removed from me now made it even more difficult to stay focused on recovery. I was angry, sad, and fearful. These feelings were magnified with the lack of the medication. This was especially true for patients who had mental illness such as Bipolarization. Some of the patients were acting out of sheer chemical withdrawal. But we were told that we needed to be able to "feel" our *real selves* and that it was necessary for the staff to observe our true emotional and mental state. This was hard to watch. There were many people who couldn't handle this. One young man stole a farm truck in the middle of the night and was gone. He went back to prison. Another called her drug dealer and was picked up from an AA meeting. She was never heard from. It seemed that almost daily someone was either leaving or acting out with violence and anger. I wasn't so sure that I would be able to stay until my recovery was stabilized, but I knew I needed to try and complete the program. I had miraculously made it through three weeks.

# CHAPTER
## 16

# GOD SHOWS UP

A large stamped envelope was handed to me by my counselor. It had already been opened because all mail had to be previewed by our counselor. The return address was from the elementary school where I had taught. To my amazement, there was a pile of cards and letters from my kindergarteners. The children had made pictures, hearts, and notes for me. I started to read them. Many said "I luv U "or "I mis yu." I couldn't look at them long before I was overcome with strong, mixed emotions. Shame and regret forced me to shove all the messages back into the envelope. The reality of my situation was starting to become clearer. The two separate worlds—that of treatment life and my regular life—were becoming evident. I had been attempting to keep these two lives separate because I didn't want to think about what I had done and how I got here. Now that alcohol was out of my system, I couldn't escape what was really happening. I was on leave and everybody in town knew that I was a hopeless drunk—even my kindergarteners. I would most likely never teach again and I certainly would never have respect in the community.

My brain wasn't doing well without alcohol. I still craved it. I had gotten so used to the normal, constant buzz. Extreme depression took over because my life was lost. I believe I felt true grief. Looking at all the loss gave way to my escape mechanism. *What would it be like to drink again? What did I have to lose? I have already lost it all!* I began to make plans to leave treatment and walk to the city. It was a few miles but I could easily make it. What then? I didn't have much money. It too had been taken away and I was only allotted a small amount. Still, I had enough for a good drunk and then I would call . . . who? Who would I call? Mary, my sponsor? Could I stay with her for a while? No. She knew better than to help me with plans of relapse. Even after this time and effort at sobriety, I still wanted to drink. It must be true after all that I was one of those who had progressed so far into mental illness that I wouldn't be able to be restored to sanity. I realized how sickeningly obsessed I was with staying buzzed. The shame was overwhelming. I still saw myself as weak and immoral instead of sick with an incurable disease.

I began to put on layers of warm clothing for the long trek to town to buy alcohol. I made the mistake of sharing these risky plans with a roommate I thought I could trust. "I'm leaving Jamie. I'm done trying. I can't do this anymore. I'm going to drink. Good luck to you. I think you have what it takes." Jamie didn't even respond. She left, slamming the door. I assumed she was angry, but Jamie went directly to the staff and "snitched." I was immediately called into the office to talk about my intent. My response was "Well, you told us to talk about our feelings, and especially how we feel about drinking so I was letting someone know."

"Have you really thought your plan through to the end to see what would happen?" The well-trained night employee asked. Of course she was right. I would end up starting all over again with the detox and withdrawal as well as reliving the painful realization that a drink only lasted for a short while and then, there I was again at the same place—only further down in the pit. There were other options. I could also die or end up in jail. I hadn't done either of those yet and I knew they were becoming increasingly possible for an alcoholic like me if I were to relapse. I went to bed without even folding the covers back or changing from all those layers of warm clothing.

I fell asleep that night after much thought about why I wasn't feeling better or even desiring to make progress. *I just **cannot** do this. Will God ever help me? Do I even love God? Yes. Does He love me? I* *guess. That's what I'm told. How? I don't get it. Maybe there is an end to how far God will go with us.* All I could think about was my horrible behaviors caused by drinking. I couldn't see or hear anything else. I especially couldn't hear that God still loved me—or that anyone could love me for that matter. I had given my life to God, but addiction had stolen my salvation away. I had thought that was impossible. *Then where is He?* I was still physically craving alcohol! I finally realized that it was God I was angry at for not making it possible for me to stay sober. I was hopeless. I decided I would leave the next day to go after alcohol.

I awoke a few hours later to a piercing voice calling out to me. "Kerry!" I jumped up. No one else seemed to have heard it. The roommates were all sound asleep. It was a voice like I had never heard. It was not a human voice. I decided that it was not audible, but in my head, although I knew that I didn't make it up. I couldn't sleep again for a while. It was a plea that I had heard. I knew "it" was asking me to stop my own thoughts and to listen. I tried to listen but heard nothing more. I finally fell back asleep and awoke again to my alarm. The impression from the voice was still there. It had the feel of a beckon or a call. I was sure I hadn't dreamed it and that I hadn't created the voice that called out my name. Even though I was depressed, I had never heard voices before. My inner self told me it was God. As I showered and went to the commons area to read, I prayed. "God, I think you're talking to me. What are you saying?" I didn't get any more vocal responses or even specific thoughts coming to me but I continued to feel pulled. I opened my Bible to a verse that said. "I knew you in the wilderness, in the land of great drought" (Hosea 13:5). That was what I needed to hear. I knew that I hadn't been forgotten, even though I felt abandoned. The message in my gut was that I wasn't really alone. Even though I deserved to be dumped by God, He had not disowned me.

I thought about the "calling voice" all day. Could it be true that God would bother with me? *I'm the worst of the worst of the hypocrites.*

That night as I got ready for bed, I felt a deep need to get down on my knees and pray an honest prayer very similar to the following;

*I have been here two months and I still don't want to get sober, God. I can't get myself to want to. If You want to try and make me want to, then go ahead. I don't think it's possible for me to get better. I will let You do the work, God. I give You my will and permission to go ahead and change my desire so that I will want to surrender to sobriety. I won't fight You anymore, but I'm pretty sure it's hopeless.*

I didn't feel confident or free after that prayer. But I did have strength to keep going. I could envision myself moving forward in small, sequential steps. The next day, I opened to another scripture that stated, "I will heal their backsliding; I will love them freely, for my anger has turned away from them" (Hosea 14:4). It seemed too simplistic that God would take me back that readily after all I had done. I had been condemning myself with constant guilt. *Was He really that patient and loving?* God had reached out to me before I had genuinely reached out to Him. I had been angry and resentful toward God.

Things didn't get any easier after those encouraging words but I was resigned to stay in recovery. I had expected early sobriety to bring feelings of relief and well-being. It wasn't about feelings. It was about *doings*. I began to pray each night on my knees—even though I still didn't want to.

Encouragement continued to come my way.

I received another piece of mail a few days later from the school system. My first response was, *Oh no, what is it now? Am I being fired?* I was sure that the envelope would contain a letter requesting my resignation. I was surprised to see that it was a letter stating that I had been chosen to receive an award called *Make a Difference.* Brianna had been in my kindergarten class and was now in middle school. She chose me as the adult who had made a large positive impact in her life! I was dumbfounded. Something good had come out of my difficult and barely sober teaching years. But then, I realized that I would not be able to go to the banquet to receive the award. My counselor Lena, however, felt that I should go. She submitted a request for me to receive a one day leave in order to attend the banquet.

"This will be too embarrassing," I told Lena.

"I want you to go," she stated forcefully. "It will help you get incentive. Remember you are doing a good thing to be here on leave. It was a difficult and right decision."

The leadership made the decision that I could leave for the evening provided I had an escort from Rayland Road along with a driver that was approved by them. *Isn't that like them to make it difficult? They didn't even congratulate me!* I began to make plans to go but realized that it would be a huge ordeal for me to go to this banquet under the circumstances of taking medical leave for alcoholism. *Does Brianna's family even know that I am in rehab for the remainder of this school year?*

"Who will I choose to go along with me? How about Leah?" I asked Lena excitedly because Leah and I were getting to be friends.

"No, I can't let you ask her. How about asking Jean?" she asserted.

Jean was an odd person but I agreed. A few weeks later, Rick picked Jean and me up for the one hour ride back to Lansfield to attend the banquet. Because I was leaving the world of treatment and going back to my *real life*, I was feeling panicked. Everyone there knew my circumstances. My pride was struggling. I couldn't fit into any of my clothes so I was wearing a frumpy dress from the donation box. At least my hair had been fixed by Leah. But Jean looked terrible and I was embarrassed by her appearance. I was also embarrassed that I had gained over thirty pounds. The evening was a blur to me because I was so self-absorbed. *What are people thinking? What should I say?* It became easier because Brianna and her family were so warm and welcoming. It was wonderful to have someone believe in you at a time like this. At dinner, we sat with a family I didn't know well and that was perfect. I could use conversational questions for new acquaintances. "What grades are your children in now?"

Thankfully Rick was a good, loud talker so he was a huge help with the uncertain conversation. "I remember you from coaching flag football back in '98, isn't that right?"

When the awards presentation began, I realized that I was expected to go up and receive the award. I would have to stand there for a few minutes in *sight of everyone*. My nerves made the time seem endless. *This is taking forever . . . I should be feeling grateful, but I really, really, really don't want to be the center of attention.*

Finally, they called me up. My legs felt weak and I wished I hadn't eaten. I stood near the podium next to Brianna and listened. I have never experienced such a mixture of high and low all at once. The words that Brianna had written to honor me were complimentary and yet, I wanted to disappear from humiliation.

*Mrs. Samulak has made a difference in my life by being one of the best teachers I've ever had. Mrs. Samulak was also my MEAP mentor. She gave me lots of extra encouragement and stuff to support me.*

Brianna was all smiles. I don't know if I was or not. First, we shook hands and then, simultaneously, decided to hug. I quietly said "And you were always an outstanding student! Thank you."

A few friends from my building came and talked with me but there wasn't much to say.

"So I miss you, guys."

"Yeah, we miss you too."

*Of course they didn't ask many questions about how I was doing.* And I felt too much like an outsider to ask them anything. To add to that, it seemed like Mr. Mann, Mary, and several other administrators were staring at me disapprovingly but that may have been my imagination. Soon it was over and I actually couldn't wait to get out of there and back to treatment. Though it was encouraging to be honored, I didn't yet feel safe at home. Rayland Road is what I needed right then.

Two months had gone by and I was entering into the last phase of the in-house treatment. It was expected that I would find a job and that I would attend social events and meetings with support members. I did finally establish friendships with some wonderful, supportive women with whom I stayed in contact for many months afterward.

I applied for work and was hired right away at a local restaurant. My job would include working in the kitchen preparing food for a salad bar and washing dishes. It was comfortable for me, but it ended up being **lots** of dishes—like heavy pots and pans—and it was hard, sweaty work. Of course, on the inside I was screaming *I'm* *a teacher! I shouldn't have to do this!* There were several other patients from Rayland Road who were working there. Sam, the young man who didn't speak for some time, was also working there as a cook. He turned out to be a kind and helpful person even though he remained fairly quiet.

During this month, several things happened to other Rayland Road residents. One, a very intelligent man with a successful career, disappeared into the city streets with his bottle and was not heard from again to my knowledge. He left behind his wife and two children as well as his recovery. A second man overdosed on his favorite drug. That was a sad and sobering funeral. Every day, it seemed we would hear of someone who threw his or her recovery away. It began to feel like a survival lottery. I am still surprised at how long the overwhelming cravings last. The substance of addiction seems to take on a power of its own. The brain is programmed for "the substance" and it has to be reprogrammed against its own will.

The psychiatrist who sent me to Rayland Road back in December was on call for those of us who needed more care. As I was getting ready to move to a three-quarter house, I knew that I needed more help. My sobriety was very fragile. I was pretty sure that I would get out of the treatment facility and relapse. I began to see Dr. Gibbs weekly. He was a huge help to me. He himself had been in recovery for years so he understood addiction from personal experience as well as from a medical viewpoint. He helped me deal with the huge amount of shame that I had acquired due to my drinking behaviors. He enabled me to understand the difference between regret and genuine repentance, as well as the connection of self-forgiveness and restitution to those I offended. Dr. Gibbs helped me understand that I needed to stay in the three quarter house facility as long as possible to gain confidence in my ability to maintain recovery. I had no confidence in myself at all. That turned out to be a good thing because I relied on God and helpful people for a while. I am pretty sure that God used this man to save my life.

I told Dr. Gibbs that I just wanted my life back. I learned that my life wouldn't be the same. It would be a new start. I began to count the cost. Do I really want my job back? Dr. Gibbs had said that perhaps I should change careers. "Teaching is a high-stress career. You need to focus primarily on recovery," he had said. That really angered me. I just wanted everything to be the way that it once was and I was grieving that I couldn't have that. I knew that with time, my family might trust me again and that they still loved me. I knew that in time I could also make new friendships. My marriage could heal, I believed. And I still had my home. I had much to be grateful for. Most people at long-term treatment had few if any of those things. I also knew that if I could work at what gave me energy and meaning, I would have motivation to stay sober. If I were to go home with no career, I would be set up for failure because I would be without the purpose and enjoyment my job had provided. Idle time would be detrimental and I couldn't get interested in anything else until I discovered whether or not I still had a job. It was now April so I still had time before next fall. Right now I needed to work hard at acquiring healthy thinking.

I moved into the next phase of Rayland Road treatment, which was three-quarter house living. This living arrangement came with a house monitor and a new set of rules as well as on-the-spot breathalyzers. While living in these apartments, I was expected to attend at least nine recovery meetings each week. I had to keep record and show documentation for these. I was starting to gain some appreciation for recovery gatherings. Fellowship with others with whom I could relate was becoming invaluable. It also became imperative for me to find those meetings at which I was both comfortable and safe enough to share my feelings. I had previously not been able to gain help from meetings because I had not wanted to recover or to try to make the necessary connections. Now I was beginning to see the true purpose and goodness in attending recovery groups. They brought both encouragement and hope for a meaningful future.

I learned more about drinking-related consequences that others had experienced. Those situations gave me appreciation for my own circumstances. Many women had obtained larger consequences than me for their drunken actions. Some had received felonies for assaulting police officers or for resisting arrest while intoxicated. I knew that I was also capable of these kinds of behaviors but hadn't experienced arrest or jail. It would likely have just been a matter of time before I did these things if I had continued to drink. Several others in the house had been presented with divorce papers while in treatment. Some were told that they had no home to return to. Though I had behaved apathetically and even abusively toward my husband, for some reason Rick didn't give up.

I had gained over thirty pounds while living in the treatment facility. I was making up for the loss of alcohol by eating carbohydrate-loaded food. I started to exercise but the weight didn't come off right away. It took three years for that to happen.

Rick and I had only been able to see each other once a week for a few hours at family visitation. During the second half of my treatment, I was able to go home for short visits. First I went for one day, and later, I was able to spend the night. Because our home had enough space, our grandson's first birthday party was celebrated at our house during this time. About forty relatives from both sides of the family came to the party. An AA support friend drove me home for the party since I wasn't yet allowed to have my car. I was not involved with any of the party preparations because I arrived just in time for the party. It was strange to be in my own home and not be a part of the planning for the event. I didn't even know my grandson very well and he certainly didn't know me. That was not what I had pictured when I became a grandparent. I felt very self-conscious. I wondered if I would ever be able to make a transition into my family relationships. *How do I start now? I don't even feel like it.* If I waited until the nine months of treatment were over, I would likely feel even further removed.

A few months later, I came home for my own fiftieth birthday party. I just kept thinking. *Here I am turning fifty and I have to be watched and given strict parameters in order to come to my own party.* I couldn't continue to harbor those thoughts of self-pity for very long. I had learned that self-centeredness was a dangerous place for my thoughts to stay. Egotistical thoughts and behaviors had become a major habit. Gratitude and altruism were a struggle to re-learn and yet, they were an important part of the answer. I attempted to focus on my family. That was when I began to enjoy the party. My one-year-old grandson became the center of attention and that was both relieving and entertaining. It was a small but important beginning.

## Kerry's Journal, 2016
### *Looking Back*

*The only thing I did right was to become desperate. It didn't seem to matter what my actions had been, as long as I admitted my neediness. My own lack of confidence and self-worth enabled me to feel the pain of emptiness that brought my surrender. Utter and complete dependence was and still is a very good thing. My motto became Psalm 57: "I will cry out to God most high, to God who performs all things for me." He did what I could not do; He changed my desire. He turned my heart. He brought hope. Confessing my weakness led me to freedom and I'm not going to give it up. I'm choosing to stay desperate.*

# CHAPTER
## 17

# SAYING GOODBYE

Saying goodbye to my roommate, Leah, was difficult. We had grown close over the four months that we lived together in the Rayland Road apartment. We had shared many things. There were times that she wanted to give up and I rescued her, and many times that she encouraged me in the same manner. There were issues of adjustment and difficulties that came with transferring to regular life that could only be understood together. Remaining sober held us to a strict, daily schedule. Because alcohol continued to have influence over us, even after over seven months of sobriety, we felt constantly apprehensive about what each day would bring, and, especially, what the future would hold. The disease of alcoholism is a force to be dealt with as if you are in a relationship with an abusive person that will never leave. You don't want to love it even though you still do. It can never be trusted, even when it continually presents itself as if it has changed for the better. *It will work this time. It will be different now.* Leah and I felt that we had beaten that evil power together. Because we had been successful in moving forward in sobriety, it was scary to be leaving each other and the facility where we had received constant accountability.

I told Leah that I wouldn't say goodbye. I couldn't. I assumed that we would stay in touch. I hoped that we would always feel that we could and would connect if need be. I didn't want to do or say anything to wreck the relationship of strength and solace.

As I loaded up my car, I had doubts about whether or not I should leave Arbor City. Dr. Gibbs and a lead counselor had both said that it would be wise to get an apartment and stay for a whole year. I had established solid meetings and support systems. Remaining a few more months would place me on the most stable ground possible. I just couldn't do what they said this time. I was at a major crisis. I knew for sure that I had to establish my recovery program near my home and the longer I waited to do that, the more nervous I became. It had been communicated to me that I needed to find recovery meetings which included women who had achieved long-term sobriety and with whom I could be mentored. I had never managed to find those kinds of groups near home. Making this transition and setting up a new support network would take guts and determination.

As I pulled in my driveway with my overloaded car, I felt lost. I was in-between two places. I called Mary, who would continue as my short term sponsor, to talk with her about the day. "Kerry, you are strong and you need to trust that you can do this." She also reminded me that I had succeeded in the city and I would be all the stronger when I succeeded in my own small town area. Not surprisingly, she reminded me to get to a meeting as soon as possible and to go every day to at least one recovery gathering.

My goal was to find a group of women that understood my intense need for stable and purposeful recovery. There was no room for error though. This was not practice anymore. This was life and death. I knew I could die, or kill someone else driving, if I didn't make it in sobriety this time. I wouldn't have access to the number of people who could help me make wise decisions and maintain priorities right away at home, but I only needed a few to get started.

I would be returning to the treatment center for an aftercare group therapy session each week. This would last six months. I was also continuing to see Dr. Gibbs, the psychiatrist, every week. He had lived through the same process himself over fourteen years ago. He knew that I needed to continue to work the twelve steps thoroughly and in a timely way. The amount of both guilt and shame that I had acquired because of drinking while living and working in a small town made it imperative that I reach the point of making amends to those I had wronged. In order to reach freedom from the constant self-condemnation, I would need to experience ownership for my actions, restitution, and clear evidence of new behavior.

The weekly aftercare group was a mixed experience for me. It was good for me to drive over an hour back to the city to attend this because it was a reminder of how far from real life I had gone while drinking. It had been necessary to remove myself from normal life in order to concentrate on treatment without distraction. Now I could see what a valuable experience it was to talk with those who had lived through Rayland Road and who were adjusting to a sober life as I was. The group consisted mostly of the same patients and staff who had been with me at treatment, so, in a sense, we were returning to a reunion.

As always, there were those who had gone back to their addiction. One woman, who had been a friend of mine in treatment, came to one of these aftercare group sessions high. She had chosen to take heroin and was assigned to go and take a drug screening test. She left insisting that she wouldn't take the drug screening because she was not high. You could never tell who would stay free and who would return to their substance. I never would have guessed that Jamie would have returned. She had been a pillar for me. And that is what made it all so scary. We in recovery can talk and act like there is heartfelt recovery going on inside, and then we can get suddenly and easily sucked back into our addiction.

At these sessions, we were trained to take one another's inventory. If we believed someone was not being totally truthful, we were supposed to question him or her and ask for specific facts and confirmation. Since all of us had a history of dishonesty—because everyone with this disease does—we had to practice being challenged to tell the truth. One person was lying about the meetings she was attending. She had made a false meeting signature sheet and was found out. A man was chasing after young women who were in early recovery by pretending to be 'helpful'. I had recognized this many months ago but had been too scared of repercussion to say anything.

The difference, apparently, in whether a person will make it in recovery is all about honesty. The *sober people* had been right after all. They had said that if there is genuine honesty and surrender to God, along with a sincere desire for help, then we have a chance to stay clean. Once an addict gets confidence in him or herself alone, we are done with successful recovery. We need God and we need help from each other or we will begin to justify complacency and will then eventually compromise. We could see proof of that surrender or lack of it by watching one another.

Aftercare was all about checking everyone's meeting schedules. Mine was especially scrutinized because I was now living at home. I talked about how hard it was to start over with new recovery meetings at home. I needed to find new supportive friendships as well as a new sponsor. Searching for meetings that provided rigorous accountability had been difficult and stressful. I told this group that I felt uniquely alone because everyone at my new meetings already knew each other and I felt like an outsider. Several in the therapy group advised me to set a goal of talking with at least three people before I left each meeting and to continue collecting new phone numbers. Calling people was very hard for me. I am an introvert and so I always felt like I was bothering people or else that they wouldn't want to hear from me. "Maybe it was just my imagination," I told them, "but the people at my new meetings don't seem accepting or welcoming. It almost makes me want to drink again!" *If I were drunk, it would be easy to talk to people.* That was how I still perceived my ability to meet and converse with new people. I was told that I had to learn to jump a long way out of my comfort zone. If these people were not going to reach out, then it was my responsibility to supernaturally become outgoing. I had to finally initiate conversation on my own. I was learning to live life without the crutch of treatment. It had to happen.

# CHAPTER
## 18

# RETURN TO LIFE

People assumed that I would not be returning to teach in the fall. I wasn't sure either. Legally, I had not been found *under the influence* while at work so I was reinstated. Since I had never failed the drug and alcohol screening, I was given a teaching contract for the year. The same zero tolerance agreement would stay in effect whereby I would be immediately terminated if I failed the random drug and alcohol testing.

As I was getting my classroom ready for the start of the year, I heard the familiar voice of the superintendent, Mr. Mann from the hall. I jumped. *Is he going to do the random testing today?* Though I had nothing to worry about, I was petrified. He shook my hand, which was clammy. "Good. I was hoping you would be here. It's good to have you back." He looked like he was on a mission; sure enough, he closed the door. His face turned stressed and uncertain. Then he said, "There will be no opportunities to take leave again without getting screened. The school board is asking about your return. Several of them, including Mr. Clark, the president, don't think you should return at all. I told them I would let you know that they have concerns and that you will be carefully monitored. Legally we have to follow the procedures that we have agreed to." I told him I was grateful for the opportunity to return, but I didn't make any response to the concerns of the board. I also had my own doubts about my return and now I would be working under heavy scrutiny and lack of support. These things were part of the many consequences I could expect in making the decision to return. But now that I was face-to-face with the administration, fear and uncertainty were taking over.

I remembered what a co-worker had said when I returned two years ago after my mandatory leave as a result of my drunken episode at the back-to-school open house. "You're not going to come back after what happened, are you? How can you do that? Aren't you embarrassed? The school board is not going to let this go." I knew she was right. Humiliation would normally be a hindrance to coming back to work after appearing there drunk. But the drive to live was stronger. If I quit work, I would have nothing to keep me from going back to alcohol. My job, in a sense, had become part of the reason to stay sober.

I had pushed the humiliation to the back of my mind. The same escape mechanism that used to keep me drunk was now keeping me from feeling complete reality. Normally, I would be so ashamed that I wouldn't want to see anyone from school again. It is a miracle that I faced another *back-to-school* open house after being away at treatment for eight months. I know now that it takes a few years to regain reality in its' truthful perspective and I can see that my desire to live was helping me survive the embarrassment. I only allowed myself to feel the shame when I went to counseling.

When the shame did come to the forefront of my thoughts, I concluded that I was probably known as *the town drunk*. If I let my imagination have free reign, I would conjure up all kinds of things that people were probably saying and thinking about me. Learning to keep my thoughts on the present time, day, and situation was almost impossible. I couldn't afford to engage in thoughts such as *What are they thinking?* My mind could easily run wild with scenarios. Those thoughts could get me drinking again to escape the humiliation. Though realistically I knew I was not the center of everyone's attention and thoughts, I fought these continuous beliefs. *Everything is NOT about me.* However, I knew how difficult it would be to avoid gossiping about someone who had returned after substance abuse treatment. If it were me on the other side, I would have a hard time staying away from *the talk*.

My work staff was wonderful. They welcomed me back and were helpful as I got ready to teach again. Church friends were also supportive. Even though I now had very few close friends because of my past self-imposed isolation, they let me know that I was cared for, wanted, and forgiven.

God was definitely at work showing me forgiveness. It was easy to tell myself that I shouldn't have another chance at my work and that I was beyond trust. I knew I deserved to be fired but since God could take me back, who was I to say otherwise? I had never loved myself—even though I was self-centered. Now I was just beginning to learn that I was valuable and worth loving. It wasn't about what I did but it was about "whose" I was and, therefore, who I am. I was desperately trying to believe these truths.

I think I may have been shielded that first year from receiving major consequences when I returned to school. I was given a class of students that were at-risk and mostly new to the district. This was done so that perhaps I would have a clean slate with parents who may not yet have heard about my past. Several parents however, did ask to have their child moved to another classroom. This continued for a number of years. Students were moved from my class list when parents discovered my history. *I may have done the same if my own child had a teacher with this disease.* I was told that another teacher was making sure that parents knew about my past. There were likely other conversations about me that I wasn't told about. Two years after my return, a student came up to me crying one day and said "My mom talks about you. She says you are a drunk." All I could do was get near her and look her in the eyes and say "I'm sorry that you heard those words. Can you see that I am okay and that I am not drunk?" She nodded her head and hugged me tightly. That had me shaking for the rest of that day.

The day came for my first random drug and alcohol screening. Mary, my boss, quietly stepped into my classroom and motioned to me. She softly said, "You need to go to the superintendent's office for testing right now. Don't take anything with you and you are expected there in a few short minutes. I will take your class." I began to feel queasy, though I had nothing to worry about. *I feel like a criminal!* As I arrived at the office, I was taken to the private conference room to meet the officer. He first instructed me in taking the breathalyzer, speaking to me like a child. "Very good. You did an excellent job!" He showed me the 00.00 results on the screen, as if I should feel proud of my accomplishment. Then, I followed him to see the rest room which, to my embarrassment, was all taped up so that I could not tamper with either the faucet or the flush handle. The water in the toilet was colored blue to make sure I didn't flush. How embarrassing! After collecting the specimen, I couldn't wash my hands! I was freaked out by that. I carried my jar of pee through the office to the conference room, wondering all the while who might enter the office. *Maybe I should just spill it!* Thankfully, the superintendent had the good sense to disappear for a while. *I thought he might join us and look at the pee too!* I was given a sanitized wet wipe, but in my germ conscious mind, that was not good enough. I watched the officer initial the tubes of pee and then we both signed a form. "Okay, you'll get the results in a few days. I'm sure they'll be fine." For some reason he felt the need to reassure me. I found myself saying "Thank you." *Thank you? Really? Yes. That is how I keep my job now. And I should have shook hands with him too. I'm sure he would've appreciated that!*

That first year I drove twenty-five miles every night after work to attend a recovery meeting or an aftercare group. These meetings had to come first, but they made my life exhausting. Regular social activities were still non-existent. But then, I didn't need free time to think either. I needed to keep listening and doing what I was told. Even the second year back, I was going to meetings at least four or five days a week. I had finally learned that I needed recovery groups, and would probably not stay alive without them.

As I continued to work with a counselor and my recovery sponsor, they were both in agreement that I needed to make amends to those I had wronged as soon as I was able. There were many things on my conscience from my drinking years that I wanted to address. Guilt and shame were continually in my face, distracting me from daily focus. Everywhere I went there were those that reminded me of something I had done. I knew God forgave me, but I couldn't forgive me, and I doubted that these people would either. I was reminded that amends would not be linked to my receiving any forgiveness. It was purely a one-sided expression. I should expect nothing in return.

When I finally got to the eighth step in my recovery plan where I could prepare to make amends, I started to write a list of people who I felt I owed admittance and restitution. There were more than two hundred names of people that I had wronged on my list. *There are over two hundred people that I can't face!* The escape mechanism started to ignite. *I simply cannot do this. Maybe I should just move away and start over. Jane was right!* My sponsor Pamela was able to give me the calmness and the wisdom I needed. She could rightly divide the true harm I had done from the normal inconveniences of chronic illness.

Pamela said to me, "If you had another disease such as diabetes, would you apologize for being gone to the hospital or for feeling ill at work? There are some things that you don't own. You have no control over time spent to get well. You only own the hurtful actions and costly setbacks that you brought to others." I was overwhelmed with relief to hear her viewpoint.

We decided together that I would express appreciation to those who had stepped in and given time or resources to those in my family or classroom. But amends are reserved for those to whom I caused personal injury. I needed and wanted to take responsibility for my actions and to ask if there were things I could do for them if they had suffered pain or trauma because of my behaviors while drunk.

Those whom I had offended might decide to pardon or forgive me, but that was not to be my expectation. I was to own and express a willingness to continue living a changed life and give them assurance that I would now build a trusting relationship with each of them if they desired that. The final list included a few business owners, several bosses, and many family members. There was one conversation that I was asked to consider adding to my amends. My daughter, Kylie, who always considers the feelings of others, reminded me that I had likely hurt my son Nolan's feelings one day at a family get together. "Do you remember how you made fun of Nolan's girlfriend Rose that time at the lake? Nolan was sitting right by you and you were laughing about Rose's looks and comparing her to a cartoon character. Don't you think you should apologize about that?" I did not remember that day at all. I had been in a blackout but I knew Kylie would remember when someone was hurt. *I can't believe I said that!* I was grateful that she reminded me of it so that I could include it in my conversation with Nolan.

Overall, the amends were a huge blessing to me because I was able to express my gratitude and appreciation for people I love. I had, in most cases, never done that. As was promised by many, these actions brought me a large amount of freedom. Every person I spoke with was pleased to hear me voice my desire to make things right. All were encouraging to my continued success. I was amazed. They had shown true grace to me.

Do I still want to drink? Sometimes I want to escape, but then I am reminded to picture what would happen if I chose to drink. The lists of possibilities are endless; I could die, or, even worse, I could kill or maim another human being. I could go to jail. I could end up homeless, friendless, family-less, and jobless. Then I ask myself some other questions. Why do I want to escape? What part of this problem is my selfishness? What part can I fix? What part can I ask for help with? What part can I give to God and get new perspective? What part can I let go of?

Drinking will only make matters worse. That is true one hundred percent of the time because I am not a normal drinker. I am an alcoholic.

### Kerry's Journal, 2015
#### *Looking Back*

*Has responsibility been removed because I'm sober? No. I am responsible for what I do now and for making amends for the past. But I am no longer **condemned** for what I did yesterday. I live in deep appreciation that someone took my prison sentence. A truly rescued person is grateful and a truly rescued person easily forgives others. If I understand this depth of payment, I will love no matter what. Thankfully, there is help for me with this. I can love because I am loved.* Forgiven means *pardoned.* Grace means *forgotten.*

CHAPTER
19

# EARLY SOBRIETY

When I was asked by a psychiatrist why I wanted to recover, I replied that I wanted to *get my life back*. His answer was, "You cannot get your old life back. Things are going to be different because you are different. When sobriety comes first, your priorities will all change." Then he amazed me further by saying, "You may not even like to teach again, at least for a while." These words caused a major resentment in me at that time. I desperately wanted to go back to my job, my home, family, friends, and church. What I really wanted was for people to all forget what I had done. I wanted everyone simply to erase from their memory what had happened to me.

Now that more than ten years have passed, I can understand some of the reasoning of the psychiatrist. This life is not like the old one. Early in sobriety, I found that I did not have the necessary emotional or social support needed for recovery because I had few connections with people. I had isolated myself from previous friendships during those years of my drinking. I hadn't truly connected with anyone during that time. Even before I started drinking, I had experienced increasingly difficult feelings about social situations. Conversing with others without numbing my inhibitions brought me major self-consciousness. This disconnection is common for alcoholics, I was told. It is a major reason for relapse. Because of that,

I had some big things to overcome. I had to overcome the belief that I was self-sufficient and that I could continue to make all my own decisions and choose my path to success. The trouble was that I still saw myself as an independently successful person even after I had proven otherwise. I had learned that I could not drink but I still did not understand that some of my thinking could lead me back to the old escape patterns of active alcoholism.

Early recovery meetings had proven to be helpful. There had also been people at the both Rayland Road facility and the half-way house who had genuinely cared. I had found opportunities while attending recovery meetings that enabled me to develop my sense of need. I hadn't known that I needed people. To me they had just become a means to get basic success out of life. Now I realized that I wouldn't survive sobriety or life unless I was able to continue to develop relationships. Could I do this outside of Rayland Road and the close-knit surrounding community? Because everyone was needy at Rayland Road, we all had the understanding that if we helped each other out, we would all benefit and maybe survive. I had provided rides to meetings and given away shoes, money, and food. They had given me a sense of belonging that I'm not sure I had ever experienced. The *Roadsters* had listened and understood.

However, when I moved back home, I found it very difficult to develop friendships at recovery gatherings. Since I was told by the rehabilitation staff and the psychiatrist that it was absolutely mandatory to find new meetings, I had to make an honest attempt. Deep down, though, I did not believe I could make the necessary connections. I had already painstakingly done this, and I didn't want to start over without the group I had known at Rayland Road. I was new to everyone at my home area meetings. They had no idea what I had been through. It would be up to me to communicate now with little or no support from *my Roadster* friends or sponsor. The people at these new recovery meetings would have no understanding of what it meant to come from a place like Rayland Road. They might assume that either I was still drinking or that I had easily gotten sober with little effort. Or worse yet, they might think that I was court-ordered to be there, which is very much what I was like because I had to collect documentation of meeting attendance to satisfy work mandates. New acquaintances might assume that I was stuck up because I was fearful. My mind was generating all kinds of predictions about the thoughts and intents of people I didn't yet know.

It did prove to be difficult to suddenly move across the state and attend all new recovery meetings. The most helpful group I found after moving back home was a combination meeting of both AA and Al-Anon people. There were other couples, like Rick and I who were also getting their marriage adjusted to recovery. Rick and I attended these together and found friends with whom we could both relate. They were free to talk about problems. They didn't try to pretend that everything in their lives was working. Even those who had been sober for many years were humble and empathetic. We learned about communication for our dysfunctional marriage. I found that I knew very little about honest communication. When frustrated at Rick, I either wouldn't speak or I would resort to phrases like *"You always do that! Why don't you ever . . .? I guess I'll just drink then!"* I learned that being right didn't always lead to happiness. I was making a small start.

It continued to be almost insurmountable to connect with people at work or at church. *Regular* people were more difficult. I relied on surface conversations and relationships. "Did you find that online?" Or "So are you from around here? What do you do?" That was pretty much the end of my part of the conversation. Real creative! I had fearfully kept myself apart. Now I was floundering desperately to carry on conversations because I had never cared enough to find out about any details of the lives of others. I was able to gradually get acquainted with people at church. I joined some small groups. When I shared my thoughts and feelings about God with others, I found that the wall of uncomfortable small talk was automatically taken down. Prayer put us on a level that required open and intimate sharing.

I had not wanted to expose my personal feelings or motives with others before. I still was selective about who I shared the inner me with. I had only tried to relate to people while I was mostly drunk and incoherent. I'm sure that this may have made it more difficult for others to trust me after sobriety. They may have experienced my slurred speech and loud, whispering behavior from previous years. I just didn't know what I had said or done earlier in the presence of most of my acquaintances. I had those worries constantly nagging at me. Everywhere I went I found myself thinking beforehand about who I might run into and what they might remember about my drunken behaviors. *Did we sit by them that time I tripped on the bleachers at the football game? Were they at our table that time I talked loud during Peter's sports awards banquet?*

I do admit that the forced small groups at rehab might have been a little helpful for me in developing some trust. Talking truthfully about major shortcomings and embarrassing situations created by me was repulsive. I was programmed to hide true motives and feelings and now I was being reprogrammed to be vulnerable. There was an instance when we played a game in aftercare group therapy where we had to respond to a written prompt about a situation where we were powerless over alcohol. I talked about what it was like to buy liquor in a small town where people knew you weren't supposed to be drinking. I shared about the many times I walked around the liquor aisle repeatedly to avoid being seen. I always bought extra items along with the liquor so that I could hide the bottles. These memories were helpful in retaining the true hopelessness of my drinking. I was reminded that I didn't ever want to go back to those days and that I must always, at all cost, stay away from that first drink. If I had one, I might never recover again.

I gradually began to develop the ability to listen to others at the after-care sessions. The ability to digest what people were telling me about their personal experience was a new skill. *Oh, that's right. I was supposed to listen instead of think about what I was going to say next.* I was attempting to care now. Caring for others is still something that stretches me. I slowly made some friends who continue even now to help me *get stretched.*

Priorities had been forced to give way to alcohol. Now my new priorities were not what I considered *normal.* It wasn't *normal* to go to accountability meetings everyday with tentative strangers. It wasn't *normal* to preface my words with "Hi. I'm Kerry and I'm an alcoholic." It definitely wasn't normal to require a *life sponsor*, or as I called it during rants, a *babysitter*. Decisions could not be made without checking my motives and feelings. *Where am I in the hierarchy of priorities? I am at the bottom of the list. It doesn't seem right.* What I learned is that I had always been the top priority and that was the problem. In order to establish healthy priorities, I had to go through painful self-sacrificing. I had to do things, **many** things which I did not want to do. What I still didn't know was that I was not capable of making balanced decisions based on a wide range of factors. Important factors such as the viewpoints of others, the good of the group, or the true unmet needs of those I affected were given deeper understanding. My own unmet needs came out of understanding the needs of others. *Students aren't getting enough sleep. Neither am I. That student is stressed and needs a break. Do I? I think he can't function because he is angry. I am too.* When I saw their need first, I saw my own clearly.

Basic priorities have come full circle. I am no longer consistently at the top or at the bottom of the hierarchy. I have learned that my priorities can actually float according to needs and schedule changes. And sometimes needs do not dictate the priority. Sometimes it is the faith to do the next right thing that becomes the first priority.

*Stop, breath, pray, hold her hand. Now what?*

Faith takes faith. I have to admit that I painstakingly learned that God is trustworthy. I did not think that were true for a while. I had felt abandoned. *Why couldn't it be easier?* When I decided I wanted to get sober, things got even harder. I believed that God didn't do His part. He didn't rescue me from *humiliation*. Those were still my thoughts and feelings when I first returned home from Rayland Road. Becoming responsible for my own sobriety felt like I was a novice being trained to run a marathon. I wanted to quit and walk. There was very little motivation. I was slow. Learning to live responsibly did not seem fair. *Couldn't I just ride along in a golf cart instead?* Responsibility proved to be part of faith. I seldom could see the whole picture but I stepped out and did what I was told. That is when I started to make progress. Walking forward and believing in an unseen destination was what I needed to do. Learning how to move in faith was important for my future.

I have learned that God is overwhelmingly good. Love and forgiveness are the things I can trust that I will receive from God. And He does fix many, many things, but God doesn't usually fix what I think he should fix. God rarely uses the timing or method that I think He should. I often require life experiences that will give me the understanding of patience. God can and will get me through my mess-ups, but He will not always give me the easy road. He knew what was best for me. My new belief is that consequences are a *God-ordained thing*. I acquired an appreciation for sobriety that I may not have had if I had been instantly delivered from alcohol. I acquired gratitude for the process of learning through living.

My family could probably receive national recognition for how quickly and genuinely they received me when I returned from rehab. They are an example of selflessness and forgiveness. I have heard of few families who compare to them in regard to acceptance of my painful growth as well as their own ability to recover from my past offenses. I cannot share the major parts of their personal stories with you. Those are their own stories. My husband, children, parents, and siblings certainly had reason to take lots of time to trust me again but apparently decided to embrace my past along with my fragile state of recovery. I saw little evidence that they were struggling. I only saw loving strength.

Mercy. That is what I received. Lots of mercy.

I deserved things that I never received. And I received more of everything good in life than I previously thought possible. I found healthy relationships. I found support, friends, family restoration, success in career, healing in my marriage, and even some peace. It has been much better than getting my life back. I've decided that I don't want my old life back after all.

CHAPTER
20

# WHAT LIFE IS LIKE NOW

After ten years of sobriety, life is much the same as before I drank, and yet, life is totally different. I have learned to be true to myself. I never had an authentic, purposeful self before I drank or while I was drinking. *Myself* was a combination of what others desired for me— or what I thought they wanted. That is why I consider alcoholism to be an emotional and spiritual illness. Though I knew that my family loved me and that God loved me, I didn't really believe I was valued.

I think differently now about substance abuse. I also see the major flaw in society's actions regarding addictions. It is a disease that requires clear thinking and focus in order to get well. You can't get better in the midst of using your substance because you don't have the necessary self-driven abilities. You can't get those attributes of self-awareness after just a few weeks of forced sobriety. The physical craving stays for months and affects all sane thinking. Sobriety cannot be gotten with discipline because that is only achieved through long-term sobriety. So it is an impossible situation. Substance abuse is different than other addictions because this addiction involves insane thinking. Smoking and overeating do not affect mental capacity. (Although I have personally understood both of those emotional addictions and have compassion for people who are addicted in those areas.) Recovery from alcoholism is like reprogramming a computer.

If it doesn't get reprogrammed when necessary, it doesn't work. It will always revert to the old program.

I have learned that people don't own me. I don't answer to them—unless I work for them. I can have my own legitimate goals and purposes. I can have my own needs, opinions, and desires. Just yesterday, I experienced something that brought this complete picture to life. I was entering a parking facility that later would require money to exit. I realized that I had left my cash out of my bag and was only carrying ID and credit. I did not want to use credit. As I was beginning to back my car up, another vehicle came up behind me. The car sat there waiting for me. Instead of giving in, which is what I would've done before, I continued to back up and motion to them. In "my previous life," I would've gone into the parking facility to appease the other driver, using credit even when I didn't want to. To most people this is silly, but to me this is a major breakthrough in both thought and action. My outward behaviors have started to match my true inner preferences. I can set boundaries. If I had been drunk, I might have even considered ramming into the car behind me.

When you don't value yourself, you don't really value others either. Though I pretended to, I didn't really know how to demonstrate love or care. The loving actions that I managed to express before *the drinking years* were often for show, which created resentment on my part. Today, I still have a long way to go in this area, but I do find myself actually caring whether someone gets help or has their needs met. For example, one day as I was leading my class out the door to go to gym class, I heard Janis crying. *Oh my gosh! What is it now? We will be late if I stop!* As I turned around, I saw her crowded up by the door with Devon, who doesn't know how to tie shoes, bending down trying to help with her shoelaces. I had to make a split second decision whether to intervene with fixing the problem or giving a quick temporary solution of "Come walk with me." I saw the distress on many faces. Some were itching to get to gym and some even wanted to leave Janis behind to let her fend for herself. Most of the kids, however, looked empathetic. The children instinctively knew the right choice. I made space and bent down, quickly tying her shoe and assuring her that she can always ask for help. It only took about seventeen seconds. In this situation, it was more important to keep the whole class waiting. I didn't feel frustrated about the waste of time and energy. I used to just go on and maybe tie it later or maybe not. Without alcohol, I can better see the difference between need and want. Sometimes children do need to figure things out on their own, but now I can confidently and effectively find a fitting solution. My snap decisions are healthier. My responses are more like that of normal, well-adjusted individuals!

Life is still hard. I have always felt different, and now I continue to do so, but I can feel myself starting to embrace those differences. I am a simple person. I believe that life is made too complex, and there is usually some truth in finding the important part and leaving the rest behind for a while; "You'd better go and use the rest room before you have an accident. Reading group will have to wait this time." That may be a silly example but it helps me to realize that order is important. I'm only ready for what I'm ready for today.

Being an alcoholic who is constantly recovering is unique in itself because it involves learning how to stay present without escaping life anymore. Feelings are not always based on truth. Often they are formed by my own false beliefs that are the result of thought patterns of self-condemnation. Sometimes my feelings are based on previous experiences which are not part of the present situation. Now I can step back and look more carefully. Maybe I will have to learn why I have those feelings or maybe I will be able to change my perspective. Are they based on what is really happening? Recently, I caught myself in one of these patterns. When I went out for a walk, I noticed that as oncoming cars approached, I looked down to avoid eye contact. *What am I being so unfriendly for?* I asked myself. The answer came quickly. *If they recognize me, the people most likely are wondering if I'm drunk.* I began to argue with myself. *It's been twelve years. Get over yourself!* I made myself wave to the rest of the cars that passed me that day. I could be proactive in this case about changing thought through behavior.

I used to believe that I was usually to blame because I was shameful. I ended up in deep depression because I was inherently inferior. *This is how I was made.* I was a loser. If it was not my fault, then I had a readymade list of who or what could be blamed.

If something gets uncomfortable or negative now, it might not be **my** fault. It doesn't have to be anyone's fault. There could actually be no one to blame; just resolution. That is definitely new for me.

Self-condemnation has been a constant hurdle in my recovery. I learned that I have looked at life through a pair of *guilty glasses.* When I was middle school age, I said "I'm sorry" to my peers all day long. Friends seemed to like my taking the blame because they felt relieved of guilt. If someone else cut into the lunch line, I would say "I'm sorry," assuming that I should've known that they belonged in front of me in line with their friends. And of course, I knew I was to blame for the drinking years. But really? Was I to blame? Today I can see that it is more accurate to say that I am responsible for them instead. I can amend my ways and I can make some restitution but reality is that I drank because I was an alcoholic. Today, even when I truly do owe an apology, I can usually conclude that I am not worth less than others or inferior just because I made a mistake. Now that I know self-condemning thoughts are usually false, I have had to make a conscious effort to stop and rethink things. Am *I to blame? How do I see myself right now? What is my part in this?* I have been taught to keep my house clean, but I don't have to own the mess of others.

Those beliefs have taken years to turn around. I am still working on them.

Staying positive is now a huge goal. Gratefulness is an important asset in my recovery because it helps me see the good attributes and possibilities in others and myself. It enables me to accept and appreciate the cost of constant recovery as opposed to becoming resentful about the energy and time spent. Ungratefulness is what leads me quickly into negativity and critical thinking. *Why did he fill my tank? I was going to get it tomorrow at the cheaper place. Aren't I capable of getting my own gasoline?* I can easily fall into those pits and stay there. Self-pity was another habitual way of thinking. *No one understands how much work I have,* or *Why don't I ever get to express anger? Everyone else certainly does and then I have to fix it all.* I'm not saying that I don't still think like that, but now I know that it is poison. It only leads to dangerous, hopeless resentment and unhealthy kinds of escape.

I am more able to look at a whole situation now. If I walk into a social event, I will notice the atmosphere, the room structure, the location of friends, family, and empty seats. I always notice whether or not there is alcohol and, if so, where it is. I do have to look for that. I don't mind if people drink who are sitting near me, but I do not like to smell the drink. That will make my stomach nervous. During the drinking years, I used to just plow my way into a reception, oblivious to any speakers, photographers, seating arrangements, or conversations of those around me. I would then either go sneak my drinks or else make sure there was always a full glass at my place. I can still be quite self-centered. I like things to be about me more often than they really should be. Maybe that will go away and maybe not.

There is no stigma, in my mind, with the word "alcoholic." I view it as a life-saving device. When I was thrown the rescue device, it included a brain malfunction manual for reinstatement. By labeling myself as an alcoholic, I could move into the new mind-set known as powerlessness. It was this label that gave me the understanding that I am not like normal social drinkers and, more importantly, I never will be. I don't like to keep the "alcoholic" label, but if I were to act on the belief that I am free and completely restored, then I may have the capacity to go and try alcohol again. This would be insane. So even though I believe that I have truly been rehabilitated, even *delivered*, I cannot—even for a second—pronounce myself forever relieved from this disease. It is important that I carry the daily reminder with me of the conniving, trickery of evil which will always look for future opportunities. For that reason I fear overconfidence. So is it an act of unbelief to still claim that I am an alcoholic? Some may see it that way, but I believe that it also takes faith to remain in recovery. It would be far easier for me to stop attending recovery meetings than to continue to give the time and energy to them. I have faith in the process of declaring our liability as one. There is great strength in the faith of the group. We know we can succeed and have beaten this horrible sickness because we have stuck together and relied on one another with God's help.

As soon as I start believing that I can stay sober on my own, I am in trouble. It is God's grace that keeps my faith and reliance in balance. I believe in what I can't see but I rely on the next step that is shown to me. That is why I take time each day to give thanks for new life and to receive the desire and power to do the things I need to do. There is something about that daily renewal that is a secret truth. A spiritual change happens each morning with that simple acknowledgement that I am rescued. I have another chance to live without condemnation. I was relieved of guilt and shame but I have to learn to believe it. I was traded, old for new. Though I have to be reminded every day that I am free, it is what I received through my desperation. Hopelessness has been replaced by a deep recognition of my need for help. This daily remembrance is also an act of submission. I have to give up my right to be in charge. I proved that I can't be in charge without accountability. What I receive then is freedom. Giving up my right to control everything gives freedom, not confinement.

CHAPTER
21

# THE PRODIGAL SON

*A certain man had two sons.*

*And the younger of them said to [his] father, "Father, give me the portion of goods that falls [to me]."*

*So he divided to them his livelihood. And not many days after, the younger son gathered all together, journeyed to a far country, and there wasted his possessions with prodigal living. But when he had spent all, there arose a severe famine in that land, and he began to be in want. Then he went and joined himself to a citizen of that country, and he sent him into his fields to feed swine. And he would gladly have filled his stomach with the pods that the swine ate, and no one gave him anything.*

*But when he came to himself, he said, "How many of my father's hired servants have bread enough and to spare, and I perish with hunger! I will arise and go to my father, and will say to him, 'Father, I have sinned against heaven and before you, and I am no longer worthy to be called your son. Make me like one of your hired servants'*

*And he arose and came to his father. But when he was still a great way off, his father saw him and had compassion, and ran and fell on his neck and kissed him.*

*And the son said to him, "Father, I have sinned against heaven and in your sight, and am no longer worthy to be called your son."*

*But the father said to his servants, "Bring out the best robe and put it on him, and put a ring on his hand and sandals on his feet. And bring the fatted calf here and kill it, and let us eat and be merry; for this my son was dead and is alive again; he was lost and is found."*

*And they began to be merry.*

*Now his older son was in the field. And as he came and drew near to the house, he heard music and dancing. So he called one of the servants and asked what these things meant. And he said to him, "Your brother has come, and because he has received him safe and sound, your father has killed the fatted calf."*

*But he was angry and would not go in. Therefore his father came out and pleaded with him.*

*So he answered and said to [his] father, "Lo, these many years I have been serving you; I never transgressed your commandment at any time; and yet you never gave me a young goat, that I might make merry with my friends. But as soon as this son of yours came, who has devoured your livelihood with harlots, you killed the fatted calf for him."*

*And he said to him, "Son, you are always with me, and all that I have is yours. It was right that we should make merry and be glad, for your brother was dead and is alive again, and was lost and is found"* (Luke 15:11—32).

In the story, the prodigal son asked for his inheritance early and took off for another country to live the *party lifestyle*. Prodigal means *wasteful*, which is comparable in my mind to living intoxicated. This son lost everything except his life while living a reckless, irresponsible, pleasure seeking lifestyle. The prodigal's lifestyle brought him homelessness, starvation, and utter loneliness. Then the son remembered his Father's household. Even the servants at home had an over-abundance of life's necessities. He decided to go home and own up to his situation. He would be willing to live as a hired man. After all, that would be the just thing since he had spent all his inheritance and brought shame to the family. He considered himself disowned. He would attempt to work out his restitution.

The father had been waiting and watching. He was filled with love for his son. He ran to him and embraced him. The father was not in agreement that his son should earn his way back. Instead, the father began to rejoice and celebrate because his son, who had been lost, was now found.

The story of the prodigal son helps me understand how God views a wayward Christian.

The father continued to hold a party for the son who had been spiritually dead, but now was again alive. The prodigal son never, ever, was considered an outcast of the family. Though he suffered consequences while he was away, he was not punished or humiliated when he returned. He did not lose his place or even his honor. His father only rejoiced. This picture is so full of how merciful God is. It is beyond our understanding. There is no one that He won't welcome back.

How and why did this happen to the youngest son? I believe that the prodigal had opened the door to deceit. *Is your father really good? The world can give you more* . . . As he became enticed by other things, he started to plan his trip away. He decided how and when he would ask his father for the inheritance. He would never have asked for that when he was younger, but now things had changed. He wanted an exciting life. He didn't realize how deep the connection with his father had become. The youngest son had always received everything good in life at home. Instead of appreciation, he demon-strated entitlement. Instead of showing gratitude, he turned prideful. The truly good things in his life were shoved aside.

Like the prodigal son, I had many years at home that were won-derful. Those were the best times of my life. The kids were at home. I was centered with them. I relied on God for strength and direction. I was connected to God and to my family. We were a unit. I spent all of my time with my children, my husband, our church, or our friends. It was joyful. It was also *bubble wrap*. I was protected and limited in my encounters. But I didn't see what I had. I didn't see that some parts of life were so valuable that I should make room for them always, no matter what.

Could it be that I got complacent because of goodness? Did I get lazy with comfort and blessings? It might be that I was already turning away from God before I ever started my career. It might be that I longed for approval of people more than of God. It might be that numbness was a better choice than seeing my motive to please people. Then came the realization that I could never please people. Shame. It all came back to that. Drinking may have had more to do with my lack of ability to see God's goodness in myself than of the busy life that took over. These are hard questions for me now because I can't re-do any part of my life. I can't pull myself away from the disaster that I was heading into. The enemy looks for opportunities to side track us. Pride and self-seeking were doors that I had unknowingly opened.

When I went back to school to earn my teaching degree, I made some difficult choices. I began to compromise away the things I loved. Since I had to stretch my time, I had to choose what to give up. Instead of giving up perfect grades and extra planning sessions, I gave up church activities. Instead of giving up committees, I gave up some family time. Instead of getting help with classroom art or decorating, I gave up my personal reading, music, and even prayer time.

Like the prodigal, I was busy starting a new phase of my life. Just as the wayward son wanted to sever all ties from his father, I was severing ties with God and my family. Just as the prodigal no longer valued the relationship with his father, my heavenly Father was no longer as valuable in my life. I was on a mission to feel good about myself.

Priorities were changing. Goal setting had become impossible so I didn't even try. I just let the pushiest, most pressing things take over. And they did take over. I am not saying that my desire to seek a career was the problem. Teaching was a calling that I believed God had given me. The problem was that I began to dismiss my own personal, family, and spiritual convictions in exchange for *moving on.*

It is clear to me now that the pulling away came first. The addiction was only the by product. I never realized before that I was starting to turn away from God before I started drinking. I had always blamed the drinking. My love to feel good about myself was what first drew me away.

I became dull to the voice of God. I didn't even realize that it was happening. His voice seemed to be softer because I was no longer listening. I was busy with good things. I was attending my kids' sports activities and music performances. I spent over sixty hours a week starting my career as a teacher. I thought I could do it all. Work drove me. It always came first. Exhaustion set in as I came home past dinnertime. I was too tired to spend time with God or my family. My special time with Him dwindled each week. Good things were happening but the best things were not happening. God was waiting for me to come and have our morning time together, but I wasn't showing up. He was patient and undemanding. His arms were always open. And God let me choose because that is what a loving father does. Then, over a short period of time, I realized that I was empty and stressed out. Life was hard and I was impatient. What was I hoping to achieve? I thought I had wanted to help children. Becoming outstanding or even the best at my job was the drive. The drive of pride; comparison of myself and others weighed me down. As those things continued to be important, I wanted an escape. It wasn't fun or fulfilling. I needed to feel better because it wasn't meeting my needs. I wasn't joyful or free. I was instead fearful and let down. I felt a deep sense of hopelessness but I tried to ignore the truth.

Gaining acceptance through success was a vicious cycle for me. It was fake love and fake reward. It was about seeking my value from man, not God. I began to feel a sense of being stolen from. I should be recognized too. *I should have been noticed for achievement when my class did so well.* Entitlement was breeding more demands.

Meanwhile, the only true caring God was speaking words of love and desire to me. I had cut off the lifeline. My creator who formed me was now second to everything. His response? He did not remove his love or care or protection. I received some natural consequences but none directly from Him. Did He send retribution or resentment? No. Anger? No.

The Prodigal son wanted new happiness. He didn't know that it would dead end and he would be empty. He envisioned himself receiving lasting joy over sensual pleasures. It is called *Debauchery.* The road down was a steep, quick thrill. But then there was nothing worthwhile. Nothing compared to life with his father. The Father **was** life. And He **was** love. And He **was** joy.

I did the same. I went after feelings. I got so empty and distracted that I sought alcohol for relief. I knew better. Alcohol and I had lots of history. I had put it to rest in my mid-twenties because I knew that I couldn't drink. Every time I drank I ended up drunk because I couldn't stop. I put the alcohol away. It was comparable to putting a poisonous snake in a box and sitting on the lid. I sat there holding the lid down for many years. I believed I had trained the snake to stay in the box. It would never come out now and if it did, it would not bite me. I wandered away from the discipline of avoiding alcohol. I began to experiment with alcohol on the weekends at first. It was exactly as I believed it to be; *I can certainly drink now. The alcoholism has left. Things really have changed.* Now I was happy and free when I drank.

I was no longer a drunk every time I drank. I was functioning and I was living an amazing life. I thought I had it all. I had alcohol, a wonderful family, a loving husband, a job where I was respected and liked, a church who loved and cared for me. For a while, I enjoyed the debauchery. For a while, I thought I had grown up.

Alcoholism was a seed planted by the enemy at an early age. I had recognized this years ago. I had beaten it during the safe years at home when I kept the lid on the box. Once I recognized the serpent was loose, it was too late. His cunning voice convinced me I was okay. He was leading me around. I was bitten. I longed for the time each day that I could be with the poisonous snake. It was alive after all.

What I did not realize is probably the most important thing about alcohol. It loves secrecy. That is the success of an addiction. It depends and thrives on secrecy. Just as the prodigal had to leave home to go after his life of private sin, so did I. If he ever wanted to return, no one would know what he had done. The son could leave space to return unscathed by his moral escapades. *No one will ever find out.* Those are the words of addiction. I also gained strength and momentum to move forward because I listened to the same voice as the prodigal son; *No one will find out how much you drink.* Those words were on constant replay in my head.

So then came the days of trying to capture sobriety again. *I will not have any wine today. It won't be able to get to me.* If I had any alcohol in the house, I would be drinking it by four thirty no matter what I had decided earlier. *I won't buy any wine and then I can stay away from it.* I would always find myself at the store at four thirty. I always got bit by the serpent. I could not get him to go back in the basket. The physical and emotional withdrawal was stronger than me. It had won. Again. Praying was reduced to confessing that I was a hypocrite and crying about the withdrawal symptoms.

The next part of the story is the most difficult; facing the truth. The Prodigal comes home. He strips himself of his rank and high standing in the community. He decides to become a servant in his father's house. The inheritance is spent. He has lived the party lifestyle and he has wallowed in the pig sty, degraded, homeless and starving.

The serpent now has morphed itself into shame. The Prodigal is forced to either die or come home. He must confess his humiliating failures. He decided to let the decision of his consequences fall upon His Father. All the way home, he rehearses what he will say to his father. How can he make any of it look good? He almost doesn't make the journey because of the shame. Brokenness is all that is left. And the serpent is laughing and taunting, *Wait until your village hears about this. Your father will be ashamed too.* The Prodigal can hear the laughter all the while he is walking home.

I had a decision to make. It was the same one that the prodigal son made. Would I drink to death or crawl back to my life and face the shame? It is a harder decision to make when a person is not thinking sanely. I was listening only to the serpent. Wise counsel sounded like nagging.

This is where God broke in and called my name out loud. His voice permeated all the other voices. I finally made the choice to face the shame and to admit defeat. I would get the help I needed. I would give myself into the care of others. And I would let my Father God decide my consequences.

God saw me coming from far off. He had been waiting and hoping. He had even been planning for my return. He could have intervened and stopped me at the beginning but a loving Father let me make the choice. He knew that I recognized His safety and care. What I was not prepared for was the mercy and acceptance. Just as the Prodigal son was given a robe and signet ring, I was welcomed. There was no "I told you so." Or "If you would've listened this would not have happened." There was complete unconditional love. He didn't want to talk about the horrible actions or behaviors. God only wanted to talk about His joy and relief. God wanted me to know I was His. I hadn't left his family as I had thought. I had left home but I still belonged to Him. I didn't have to beg to get back in. What kind of a God does that? He came after me and called my name during my worst and hopeless night when I couldn't make myself want to get well. He watched and waited for me to return. He Himself was moving on my behalf to let me know that I was loved and wanted.

The reason that it took me so long was that I did not think that I should be able to come back easily. I believed that I had to earn my way. It didn't make earthly sense that I could just return without payment or punishment. I deserved condemnation. But I was still His. He Himself had earned the way for me. What I had done was forgiven. He Himself gave me the desire to return. I had asked Him to change my will but I didn't expect anything to happen. *God doesn't go against the will of those he loves, does He?* But He knew I was ready to turn back. At the exact right moment He showed up and reminded me that I was His. He said my name.

I couldn't see how much I was loved because I had been blinded. Finally I realized God never left even though I felt like He had. He came with me to the treatment center in a tangible way. It was His idea to come. God didn't follow me there out of obligation but He came along out of love. He waited patiently. He called out to me when He knew I was ready. I could slowly begin to have gratitude for God being who He said He was; a Savior and Redeemer. Though it took time, the resentments began to be put to rest. They died just as He died for me.

I see now that there was no way I could've turned back to the Father on my own. It was only the Father who could bring me there. I couldn't change my own wayward heart. It was He who helped me feel His love. It was He who enabled me to forgive myself and to receive His forgiveness. It was He who helped me to hear His voice calling me. It was all His doing. It was all His grace.

# CHAPTER
## 22

# GROWING UP AS AN ADULT

Many things happened the year I turned six. I missed half of my year of kindergarten because I had mumps, measles, and scarlet fever, followed by chicken pox. On my sixth birthday, my tonsils were removed. The attention of being sick became important. I got TV, popsicles, coloring books, prizes, new slippers, but especially attention. When I went to treatment for alcoholism, I noticed that I liked to be nurtured by caring staff. I was reminded of my sick year of six. I stayed in bed and my family checked on me. People talked softly by the door about my progress. I woke up feeling confident I would be individually cared for. And I especially loved being given medicine in the middle of the night. My parents disrupted their schedule to see that I was given my prescribed amount. They had to set their alarm to come in and bring it to me. I was loved. At treatment, I felt loved again when I was given care. Even though I had behaved shamefully and drunken the night before, people showed kindness to me, not because I deserved it, but because I had needs. I was forty-eight, and those same needs were getting met. When I realized I had those clear memories and feelings of my sixth year, I also realized that the past certainly does trigger our present feelings and beliefs.

Other memories do not carry the same positive effects. I am noticing that resentful memories carry bitter feelings, and bitter feelings often stay unresolved. They pop up when a similar situation brings that familiar feeling back. Over forty years later, I found myself responding to a memory of my year of six.

On Easter, we had an egg hunt at my grandma's house. Adults helped the younger children find eggs. My siblings, cousins, and I who were close in age, were considered old enough to fend for ourselves. As we were gathering eggs from the bushes, yard, and porch, I kept hearing aunts, uncles, grandmas, and grandpas excitedly yell out clues. "Go look under the chair, Reagan! Can you reach it? Look by the swings, Danica! There's one by the slide! "The two young children would laugh and run to get the egg that they were directed toward. My siblings and cousins who were near my age were running fast, scrambling to get all the eggs before I got there. It didn't occur to me to go and look somewhere else. I was focused on their egg gathering. *They keep getting them all! I don't have any! Jay has lots already!* That only made it worse. I started to cry and couldn't see clearly anymore. When we went inside to count them, I was hysterical. "I don't have any . . . Any! They kept taking them all before I could get them!" I was sobbing uncontrollably. Though we all got candy for prizes, I couldn't let go of the injustice of having gathered no eggs while everyone else got plenty. Some kids even had help. I received no help. Grandma saw that I couldn't control my emotions. She felt sorry for me. "Here, Kerry, come and see what I have on my shelf over here." She took my hand and led me to her shelf of knick knacks. "Do you like the birds? You did such a good job trying to find eggs that you deserve a special prize. Pick out your favorite thing to take home with you." My disappointment had been understood by Grandma. She saw how unfair it had been. I was appeased and somewhat relieved that I had been understood. But then, I heard snickering from the corner of the room. Lana and Denny were laughing about my crying episode. "Oooh, look at Kerry. Now she gets the birds. Cry, cry, cry. Then you'll get what you want!" They had waited for the adults to leave the room so they were not heard. I knew what they said was somewhat true, even though it was mean of them to make fun of my emotions. I began to believe that I deserved to be teased and made fun of. I left the room and went to sit with Mom and Dad at the table. I never told on Lana or Denny because they were partly right. Therefore, I must be wrong. I felt guilty and ashamed.

Forty years later, when I was given a perfect attendance award at work, I immediately heard whispering from the other table. A few teachers were talking about how unfair it was that some people got awards for attendance. "We can't help it if our kids were sick and we had to use our sick bank. Everyone who got one of those attendance awards doesn't have young children!" Though that is true, I felt cheated out of my rightly earned award. I became embarrassed that I received the award. *I didn't deserve it. I guess Annie is right.* But then, the Easter egg hunt memory kicked in. *We shouldn't be honored because she has sick children! Even though I already raised my children, my accomplishment should be ignored because she now has children? I had my turn to have sick kids too!* Here came the sarcasm and the resentments full force.

I felt the same anger bubbling up from inside that I had felt when I didn't find the eggs. I was made fun of for crying and getting the china birds. My reception of good was squashed by entitlement and jealousy of others.

Now I realize that the sober people in recovery who said that resentments are why we drink, may be right. The story about egg collecting is a simple example of how resentments hang on. Angry, bitter thoughts get stuffed down inside and keep reappearing. Every year we rehearse the same lines, feel the same feelings, and believe the same bitter injustices. Worse, we pile up more on top of the first, because each one is felt more deeply. The path was made. I kept on trampling over it, making it more pronounced. *I guess I don't deserve it, I guess I don't deserve it, I guess I don't deserve it.*

Resentment is the greatest enemy of sober thinking. Gathering anger while stockpiling past issues is how many of us who are in addiction lived. Dwelling on unfairness was ingrained. It became a habit and when we could no longer deal with the anger, we drank or drugged to get away from it all. I didn't used to believe that. I figured I drank because I liked the buzz. Then I decided I drank only because I was an alcoholic. I see now that those people were correct who counseled me to take a long look at my complaints and grudges.

I was even more shocked to see how long they remained after I was sober if I allowed it. Recovery from addiction may be compromised if resentments are not let go. The habitual ways of harboring resentments have to be destroyed and completely redirected. It is time to grow up.

Over the twelve years of sobriety, I have gradually dealt with the patterns of bitterness from my past. Comparison and greed for recognition were huge hurdles to overcome. Some are obvious circumstances like having your friends, siblings, or co-workers excel and receive praise while you get used to being overlooked. At first, I tried to think about what really happened. *Was that even true that I was overlooked? She really is that friendly and helpful. She does deserve that award. Besides, showing up for work hung over and unprepared does not qualify one for an award or for professional respect.* That helped but I still felt angry.

*Who is the best or most worthy?* I still get hung up on comparison sometimes. I struggled to believe that there was no favoritism with God. I have always thought that God preferred others over me. I had messed up so I would be rejected. Even before I started drinking, I believed that I was loved less. I was not worthy of God's love because I was not as wise, as holy, as competent, or as dependable. I deserved to be loved . . . yet I was unworthy. False perception of inequalities brought resentment.

I believed that God favored the newly saved addicts. They had come to Him and were set free and received salvation. They did things in the right order. They were grateful for His redemption. Those people deserved to be loved by God. They belonged to Him **after** the drunkenness, **not** during. I was also resentful of the ever-faithful ones who never left God. He especially loved them more. They were His beloved. They were the ones who did the good deeds and showed up for everything.

In part, this was why I drank and in part this kept me drinking. When I wanted to get sober, I thought God would never help me because I had turned my back on Him. I hadn't tried very hard. He wouldn't want me again if I did get sober. I wasn't loved as much so I drank and then I wasn't loved or wanted **because** I was a drunk. I listened to the voice that said, *God will never want you again. He loves them more.* I had to pray to overcome these false beliefs.

It is amazing how fast God can turn these impaired and immature attitudes around once I see them clearly and surrender them. Freedom for me came through God's healing. He used many avenues to help me. Working the twelve steps led me through the sorting out of true wrongs from the falsely perceived hurts. My mind has had to dig deep to consciously find the lies that I believed.

Receiving mercy was a new experience for me. It is not just for the deserving few. Forgiving others and receiving forgiveness was new. Giving kindness and mercy to *me* was also new. Picking up rightful ownership of my intentional vengeful actions was new. Laying down past ownership of circumstances beyond my control was also a new experience.

Counseling is another thing that reformed my thought processes. **Stop**. *What are you thinking? Is that really true? Why do I feel this way? What need of mine did not get met? I can't believe that I've had that perspective all these years!*

Freedom also came from realizing that there are many things that I could and should have done that I failed to do. I own the responsibility for the times I ignored the voice that told me to apologize or to "right" an injustice that I had created. I hurt others through neglect. I was absent in spirit though present physically. Sometimes I was even absent physically or not desired present because of my behavior. So I've had to figure out answers to many questions. *What is my part? What was my true motive? To whom do I owe an amend?* Amend means that I turn my behavior around and actively make restitution for my past hurtful actions.

Other patterns of resentment were much harder to scope out such as the belief that God Himself treated me unfairly because He allowed me to suffer sexual abuse. That is hard to admit. I was a victim. I won't diminish the pain and suffering, but thinking like a continuous victim is something that had to be overcome. It was important for me to purposefully seek to forgive. The person is not the enemy. Evil is the enemy. That is my personal conclusion which brings gratitude for my survival. At first it seemed natural to dump the experience of abuse on God. But God is good. I believe He only does good things. The world has an enemy who is evil. Some people choose to follow evil. Some people choose to do horrible things to others. I continue to process these events.

I am **not** *what happened to me*. What happened **to** me are hurtful events. I am still who God created me to be.

Resentment can be a problem even now if I choose to go there. I hate injustice. If I believe that I or someone I care about was treated unjustly, then I am tempted to get resentful. One example took place a short time after returning home from Rayland Road. I was talking with my daughter Samantha on the phone. She casually said, "Oh, I had a terrible headache Wednesday so I called Jessie at six in the morning to come and get Kevin. I don't know what I would've done if she hadn't been able to take him." I was filled with rage that I wasn't asked to get my grandson but my rehearsed responses took over. I found myself saying, "Oh! I'm so glad she came and helped you out." When I got off the phone, my resentful thoughts wouldn't quit for a long time. *Why didn't she even consider calling me to go over and help? Did I get sober for nothing? Am I ever going to be trusted again to spend time with grandchildren?* After a few hours, and a talk with Pamela, my sponsor, I knew that it was right for Samantha to call Jessie, her mother-in-law. *It will take time. It takes time to build trust; especially when the safety of grandchildren is involved.* Other situations that were ripe with seeming inequity happened over the years of recovery. People were used to my apathy and distance so they couldn't immediately embrace my recovery. It rightfully had to be proven over time. I had to learn to talk and process the resentments with friends, sponsors, and God. I had to let them go. I had to stay honest. *Later* is when I would understand. *Later* is when I could see clearly. I wouldn't get better if I didn't learn to wait until I processed things carefully.

Resentment is a choice. If I am wronged or feel cheated, I can choose to look past it and learn why or what my options might be. I can follow the grace and make peace. Forgive as I was forgiven. Even this is only done with the help of God. It's very easy to go back to entitlement and bitter envy. *Why didn't I get invited to go out to lunch with Donna? I suppose that I have to remember that I have excluded and abandoned her before.* I tell myself what I tell my first graders, "She can have more than one friend. A person can have lots of friends." *God please help me with this.*

Resentment is always an important choice—maybe a life or death choice.

The greatest reprogramming for me has been learning to think on the good things instead of the negative. Gratitude is a novel idea for me. I have not won this battle yet but have made some good progress. Years of looking at what was wrong and at what was missing had become habitual. I could choose to see myself as an introverted, second-class citizen with a fear-producing, debilitating disease. The other side of that is to see myself as an overcomer who has gained access to hope and grace. It is also important to see myself as a patient with a horrible disease which is now in remission. I could choose to see my community as a place of constant shame because I might still be known as *the town drunk.* But I can make the opposite choice to see my community as the place where I grew up as an adult. I could see my husband as a loser because he stayed with me or I can see him as a courageous and wise husband who believed when no one else did. Pieces of both perspectives constantly pop up and I have to choose in an instant.

Resentment believes that little was given even though all was deserved. Gratitude believes that little was deserved and all was feely given.

Gratefulness overpowers and even reverses negative selfish thinking. It almost seems too simplistic but it is true. Though gratitude is one small change in attitude, it was difficult for me to make that change. But the results of taking time to painstakingly concentrate on it bring big change in outcome. *Thank you, God, for her patient, helpful friendship. I am blessed to have worked with her. Thank you Lord that I was able to keep my job.* Once again, I could not do this myself. I had to get help from God and others. Friends in recovery and church have been amazingly helpful and non-judgmental. Sharing uncomfortable feelings is worthwhile and strengthening in the long run. We no longer feel weak and alone once we tell others. Though we can't do it alone, the work is up to us alone.

One of the most difficult ways that I have had to fight to grow up is my beliefs about myself. How long would I consider myself to be inferior? It has been twelve years since I returned to sober life. I still fall back into thinking of myself as *less*. I have had this issue most of my life, but it grew worse during the drinking years and even worse yet in the post-drinking years of reality.

Now I am picking up the debris and starting over. I used to think it was humble to see myself as *less*. Now I see that I am merely remaining impaired emotionally if I believe I am still less. I have been relearning how to feel, think, and behave as a person who believes in my own worth. *Don't just erase. Get a new paper!* It is as though I need daily parenting. Does the world need more child-adults? There are already far too many adults who behave as children. *How long will I continue to view myself as worthy of rejection because I drank over a decade ago?* The good news about this is that I am ready for change. I am hungry to move on. I have role models and I have wise counsel. I now have faith in the process of healing because I see it work in so many other brave individuals every day. I can see the tiny increments of growth I make each day if I look for them.

Self-rejection meant that I had little to give to others. My mind stayed fixed on meeting my own needs. I looked only at what I needed from others.

I have begun to truly desire to help others. I still require lots of support and encouragement though. If I help someone, then I sometimes want recognition for giving that help. I am learning to allow God to be my rewarder instead of people. I find that having a close friend or spouse who can give occasional necessary encouragement is helpful. That person can point me to God and say, *Look what God is doing in you! That is amazing how you found a way to help that family.* God still gets the credit and I also get some needed feedback to keep me going in the right direction.

God pursued me when I was lost in alcoholism. He viewed me as worth rescuing. He goes out to find the lost sheep. He carefully delivers one lost sheep at a time. Another similar biblical parable is about the woman who sweeps her floor looking for one lost coin. She rejoices greatly over the one lost coin. These parables, along with *The Prodigal Son* are included in the Bible for a reason. He loves those of us who stray from the rules of life, those who hurt and hurt others, those of us who bring shame upon Christianity, those who have disdain for ourselves. But He doesn't want us to stay lost in those shameful memories or behaviors. The way has been cleared.

Can I see that I'm worth rescuing? Yes. I have gradually learned that I am worth rescuing. God made me. He created my temperament. He planned me. He bought and redeemed me. My mess ups can even be used to help others who have mess ups. Nothing is lost or wasted. He even knew that I was going to do all that awful stuff. That one is beyond my mind.

A mature adult forgives. I finally forgave me. I looked in the mirror one day and said, *I forgive you, Kerry.* Simple maybe, but it was much harder than it sounds. It was a big first step that started things moving. I had to say it for a number of days before I started to believe it.

It is time to find out what God believes about me. There are good readings, like Psalm 139, that depict how God knew me and planned me before I was born. *His thoughts toward me are more than can be numbered* (Ps. 40:5). How do I come to believe those things? First, I meditate on the scripture, and pray for a renewed mind. Secondly, I try to appreciate one thing about myself each day. And lastly, I try to appreciate one thing about someone else.

Daily affirmations have made a difference. I take quotes with me in my pocket every day. Sometimes I memorize an encouraging word from another person. It is simple, but not always easy. What happens when the remarks of people or my own thoughts argue with these affirming truths? It happens regularly. I recognize the negative and actually tell those thoughts to stop bothering me. It works. I may have to do it a number of times but it changes my thought process. It creates new responses and beliefs. The enemy would like me to believe that I need eighty years of counseling before I can have some freedom. I mostly need the inner voice of the Holy Spirit to direct me and I need to be obedient.

Being an adult means that I become nurturing. Nurturing is an important concept in maturity that I had overlooked. Caring for others means that I am more than a recovering, forgiven Prodigal. I am now a forgiver of others. I am more than a wayward child for whom Christ suffered. Because He suffered, I can become patient, empathetic, and kind—even when I am boiling with anger. If I yell or criticize, I apologize. I admit when I am going the wrong way again. This sounds a little like an elementary social studies lesson. But I am an adult and I am a Christian. An adult Christian is always moving toward becoming Christ-like. I often look for more complex solutions and overlook the obvious next right thing. A child can help me remember my way; *treat others the way you want to be treated, find the puzzle piece with the sky first, take a breath.*

I have an unusual story. But not really. There are many stories about drunks and there are many drunks. The stories are only valuable when they help another alcoholic see the truth about themselves. I am not unique. Pride about being a recovered drunk is a trap of getting me to stay stuck on me. I'm truly unique only in ways that are divinely given. God loves the funny, interesting, and small things about me and about you. But he does not love the *drunk* stories. He loves our gifting that He placed within. If you are one who enjoys finding ways to show love to people, it is because God gifted you with that. If you are one who loves reading or writing, it is because God gave you those interests and abilities. If you are one who loves driving, running, cooking, or taking care of babies, God gave you those desires. God has given me opportunities to help other addicts get freedom. That is a process that I enjoy being a part of. There is nothing more satisfying than to be a partner with God in helping. Sometimes He uses our worst problems and faults to eventually bless others with understanding and freedom.

That is called growing up.

There are millions of people who need encouragement. Those who have sifted through their own strengths and weaknesses can empathize or answer a question like no one else can. Encouragers often have scars of their own. Scars make fruit. There are millions who need to be nurtured and shown mercy. Those who have that gift are called to share it. That is what God made us for. That is what God loves. We don't need years and years of preparation to hear God tell us to help someone. He needs us because people need us. That is the spiritual part of recovery. God gives freely and I can too.

# CHAPTER 23

## SPEAK AND YOU WILL LIVE

I had a dream about a ravine filled with black body bags . . .

I began to wake up. I felt the sweaty plastic and the wet dirt plastered to my body. Then I remembered that I was inside one of the black body bags that filled the huge ravine.

There was a heavy force of deep sleep inside me. I felt overpowered by the voice that said, *Give up and give in . . . This sleep is the only thing that will bring relief. There is nothing else now but to give up. Dying is good. You can't win. Relax. You tried to fix this but it is too late. Just close your eyes and your mind. I will do the rest. Go back to sleep . . . go back to sleep . . . go back to sleep.*

There came an urging that I intrinsically knew was the Savior. He didn't speak in words, but used the *inner knowing*. I was compelled to fight the sleep. I felt the battle in my weak body. The battle against the two forces was making it more difficult than ever to avoid the sleep. I wanted relief. Apathy and resignation versus the divine power of the Savior were the choices. There was no doubt that the Savior was greater. His power would come to me if I continued to lean toward Him. I would get strength as I followed . . . I would be pulled to rescue as I gave myself to His drawing. As each second went by, I had to determine not to succumb to the loud, easy words of the enemy. I could not do both.

Suddenly I became aware of forces outside of my bag. The same war was raging in the other body bags that filled the ravine. But higher still, outside the ravine, I sensed the same two forces again. There were prayers of saints going up to God's throne for those individuals who had been thrown to their death. There were those in God's army who were fighting in prayer for the defeated saints in the body bags. Some intercessors cried and groaned. Others could not speak, but just remained in silent anguish before God. They, too, felt the urgency of God's call.

There was also the voice of the enemy taunting and triumphant. "I have won! I have brought these believers to the ground. They are too weak from addiction. Let us continue with our words of hopelessness to those in the bags! Let us continue with our voice of complacency to those in the church."

That is when I heard the Savior's words to me: "**Speak and you will live!**" Though He spoke only five words, His message contained truth, life, and power. The *knowing of the Spirit* told me to declare forth the greatness of God. The *knowing of the Spirit* caused me to proclaim my own deliverance through His resurrection power. The *knowing of the Spirit* brought encouragement to my mind. "I have overcome because greater is He who is in me than He who is in the world" (1 John 4:4). *My own testimony is that God is far greater than any addiction.*

I tried to open my mouth to speak. It felt permanently closed and dry. I finally parted my lips slightly, but the fight was so difficult that I was again overwhelmed with the sleepy temptation to quit. **Start saying the words in your head!** came the voice of the Spirit. *I have overcome . . . Greater is He . . . who is in me than He who is in the world . . . I have overcome.* Then my voice began to press out of my throat, one word at a time; I . . . have . . . over . . . come. It was only a whisper at first.

There was still the strong temptation to sleep. The hopelessness was trying to force its way back in. Its power was not easy to cast off. *God help me do this!*

I felt a strength that enabled me to force myself to focus on speaking the words of the Savior. My voice began to come. It was stronger each time I repeated the phrase. "I have overcome . . . I have overcome . . . I have overcome."

But would I ever get out of this body bag? I realized that the zipper was on the outside of the bag. *How will I ever unzip it? Is it still possible for a miracle?*

I knew that this ravine was part of the enemy's major plans. Many of us who had chosen addiction were now in the ravine. We had been thrown over to our death. Alcohol or drugs had been our God.

Would He come rescue us? I waited, silent now. I heard nothing but my own panting. I felt the tears wetting my face and hands.

From far across the ravine I heard one voice echo. "I am Riley. I am an alcoholic." A second voice nearer to me began to cry out. "Our Father, who art in heaven, hallowed be Thy name."

I instinctively joined in. "Thy kingdom come. Thy will be done on earth as it is in heaven."

I heard the prayer partner near me shout. "I see light! The light is shining on me! I'm coming out!"

Across the ravine, I heard the voice of Riley say, "I am free!"

I continued to pray. "Give us this day our daily bread and forgive us out trespasses . . ." Was it my imagination? There was light appearing at the top of my bag. The stream of light continued to widen until I could see all around me. I saw the filthy man who had been praying with me. Covered in slime and mud, I could only see his red eyes. He was jumping up and down and crying out. "I'm free! I'm really free."

My own bag began to fall away. I unfolded my shaky legs and tried to climb out. Great fear pulled at me. I was terrified to be outside of the bag that had been my cocoon. Boldness and joy swept the bag out of the way as I realized there was nothing to fear anymore. I was as filthy as the man who first started to pray. I found myself jumping up and down with him. "My name," he sung out, "is John!"

"And I'm Kerry."

I was stunned by the enormous piles of black body bags. It was a larger place than I had pictured. It was a canyon! Were there more people in these bags that were alive? The inner knowing said yes.

Again I felt the urgency of the Spirit. I knew I had to quickly try and make my way to the edge of the canyon. The other two, John and Riley, who had been the voices in the bags were also struggling to make their way through the piles of bags. The silent bags contained those who would also have to make a decision of their will. I was not able to give help with that choice.

I looked up to the edge of the great canyon and realized that it was a straight wall. We would never get out. I heard the enemy again. "What are you bothering for? There is no way out. You will die here as I told you already."

My heart dropped. My knees buckled. I felt sick and sweaty again.

Then I heard more voices from the top. I saw movement. There were about ten people gathering, shouting from the top edge. They were standing, cupping their hands over their mouths and shouting down. "Come here! We will pull you up! Come over to the side. We can get you!"

"No!" shouted the enemy. "It's not possible!"

*Was he right? How would it be possible to get up the vertical wall?*

John was pointing and signaling to me. "Look, a rope! Come over here!" There came a thick rope dangling down the side, inching its way to John. He expertly made a knot and sat on it. The group at the top pulled slowly and steadily. They were almost done getting him to the top when I heard cheering and saw more people gathering around those who had been leaning against the rope. They were throwing it down to me! John had made it out! I turned to see the other person coming from far over the ravine. It was a teenage girl. I knew this was Riley, who had spoken earlier. "Come on Riley! We can get out!"

I was almost to the rope when I was certain that I had heard whispering from a nearby bag. My heart jumped. Someone was giving up their will. *Oh, please God, let them cry out for your help!*

I shouted out to the area from where I heard the whisper. "Yell out the words that you hear in your head! Call out to God! You can get out! Tell the world you are free! The bag will come off if you speak the words!"

I saw slight movement from a bag but heard nothing more. *Pray for him!* I heard the Savior say. "Yes, Lord, I ask for mercy and strength for this one in the bag. Deliver this one from the evil of addiction! Give them the will to cry out!"

I heard a voice from the moving bag. "I'm Dean and I'm powerless over alcohol. Here, God. Take it. Take my addiction!" Then he began to sing, "All the way, my savior leads me . . ." His head emerged with joy on his dirty, tear streaked face. He began to crawl to the rope.

I got on and held the rough rope tightly. It was difficult to stay on but I wasn't about to let go. I kept bumping against the dirt wall as I jerked with each pull. My hands burned and my arms shook. I could see Riley standing below me crying. At the top were more gathered who were pulling, praying, and eventually grabbing for me as I reached the edge. I was overcome with the joyful knowledge that this spiritual unity was what won the fight. As they parted to help the next one, I saw thousands rejoicing and dancing in the grass.

*This is the gathering of those who spoke out!*

I saw groups of people talking and laughing together. These were the rescued who were now the rescuers. Some individuals were speaking to large groups, sharing their strength, hope, and truth about freedom from the evil lies of addiction. Other groups were praying. I knew the prayers were for those still in the pit. Prayer was the only thing that could free those from their death sentence. They must surrender their will. Those in the body bags must speak out their individual words of freedom.

God alone delivers. He uses our own confession to accomplish this deliverance. We in addiction can get out of the body bag if we confess our need to God and to others.

It was my experience that getting to this point of surrender was one of the most difficult things I ever did. I clearly felt a dark spiritual restraint when it was time to let others know about my alcoholism. I knew that I had to get help and admit my defeat. I also knew that it had to be me that did the speaking on my behalf. No one else could do it for me. There was a positive spiritual release by my own words going forth.

It was more than likely that the prayers of persistent, faithful, individuals allowed me to hear the message and gain courage to speak so that I could remain alive.

I believe that addiction is a spiritual and physical deceit that requires both spiritual and physical response. The constant thoughts of defeat and hopelessness require extreme intervention. The spiritual actions are acceptance of denial followed by speaking out deliverance. This involves dispelling and confessing the lies that have been long held feelings and beliefs; *I am beyond hope . . . I believe that I do not deserve to live . . . I still want to drink . . . I don't even feel like I believe in God or in people who are supposed to be good.* My own new words became a prayer of confession; **"God help my unbelief of Your goodness. I admit that I've wanted to die. Please forgive me for following my pride and the enemy instead of You. I have loved alcohol more than anything else. Change my heart."**

An important part of recovery is that we confess our faults to one another. Speaking our own words is vital. Then we must also encourage and pray for each other. The healing comes through those two actions. I could not get sober on my own. Others who believed with me were the important key to my freedom. We confessed to one another our addiction problem without making excuses or leaving anything out. Complete truth was mandatory. We asked God for help and strength. I received His forgiveness for my destructive testimony of a Christian life. My amends to others would come later.

I have gotten free. The enemy cannot successfully accuse me any longer—unless I allow it. It can be a daily walk of refusing the shame. Telling about my freedom is what keeps the freedom.

As I mentioned earlier, I already had given my life over to Christ before I started drinking alcoholically. That is why I thought I was hopeless and beyond rescue. It wasn't supposed to be that way. If you were born again, then you lived a changed and exemplary life. Dependence of substance is unacceptable to the Christian lifestyle. I was saved and I could not live without alcohol. That is a position that draws criticism from most people and it especially draws deep condemnation from my own self. Some might say, "That is not possible, is it, to be in a relationship with God, and a constant drunk at the same time?" Being a drunk while claiming to know God seems hypocritical, but yes, it is possible and overwhelmingly true that God loves and forgives, even during our time of unfaithful and even blatant disloyal actions. He maintains His part of the relationship because He is faithful. God, in His mercy gives more than just a few opportunities. God does not say "Oh, you're too late. You missed it by just one too many drunken episodes. Your time was up." Should we judge God by the motives and beliefs of human beings? In todays' culture, we worry about fairness and justice. Because of this, it doesn't seem acceptable or likely that there is a God who loves us unconditionally. I believe that this is what makes people dislike Christianity. We are favored people, though not because of our goodness, but God's. It just doesn't seem right to society in general that we, who are saved, can have moral imperfections and, yes, even huge purposeful self-serving offenses. The evil one loves to point out that we are hypocrites and to draw attention to our earned criticism. He applauds and leads the procession of finger pointing. Satan fights the hardest against those who have found the truth. And it really is a spiritual war. The enemy wants us humiliated, devastated, and dead so that we can do nothing for God's kingdom.

A Christian has the added problem in their addiction of keeping it quiet so no one will find out. *I'm supposed to be above this kind of thing,* we think. We don't want even our best friends to know about our alcoholism because we fear that we will lose them. In truth, we have already lost most of our closest relationships when we chose drinking over them time and time again. That means we don't ask for help. We are alone and isolated because we can't tell anyone. We worry about what others will think so we continue on in our cycle of hopelessness, physical illness, isolation, and fear of being found out. Instead of speaking truth, we stay in the body bag.

I certainly felt abandoned by God and everyone when I was continually drunk. The enemy knew this. He would fill me with thoughts of rage about how abandoned I was. Resentments piled up. But what does God say about this? *I will never leave you nor forsake you* (Hebrews 13:5). Jesus was forsaken on the cross so that I will not be forsaken. Neither am I abandoned nor was I ever abandoned by Him. He was there when I cried out to him with nausea and the DTs. He was there when I couldn't leave the toilet. He was there when I couldn't look in the mirror. He was there when I got down on my knees and begged Him to help me. When I stood up from my prayer with tremors and grabbed another bottle, He was still mercifully there. I sense now that He was heartbroken.

There is another problem with admitting defeat to an addiction when you are a born again individual; churches in general struggle to understand the unique challenges of addiction within the Body of Christ. It is just not supposed to happen if you are saved. Many Christians believe that we could quit if we were self-disciplined. Some question our salvation and wonder if we are really saved. Finally, the biggest misunderstanding is the accusation by some church goers that if we are in addiction we are abusing grace. Some Christians think that we are purposely living in addiction because we know that we are saved and that *God's grace will cover us so why would we bother to get free of our addiction?* The accusation is that we addicts think we are going to heaven anyway so we might as well drink or drug. To that I say that we can't abuse grace if we think that we no longer have it. People in addiction usually believe the lie that we have permanently lost the love and forgiveness of God. We feel we are not good enough for God or the church. The truth is that addicts and alcoholics need to be fed love and care. Some are at the point of mental illness and suicide. Most of us have a wound of some kind and cannot cope with the memories. Many of us cry out to God night and day and ask for help. We think that it is too late. We listen to the enemy who tells us that it's over and that cases like ours cannot obtain sobriety; *You are too crazy, sick, and hopeless.* We believe that the grace ran out for us and we are doomed. We are ready for our lives to end in this torment. Many alcoholics and addicts choose to end their own lives. Should we be criticized by those who know God's mercy? It is my hope that the church will join in with the efforts of those who are rescuing the addicts from the pit of body bags.

No two stories of recovery are exactly the same. That has been important for me to remember. If we compare our own experience with others who got well quickly, we blame ourselves for the slow progress. Some of us prayed to be freed but still remained strongly addicted for a long time. As I mentioned earlier, many people do get immediately delivered from their addiction! These cases are miracles and may God be praised. It is unfortunate, however, that those of us who prayed and did not immediately receive that freedom sank even deeper into the pit of despair as we compared ourselves with them. We believe that we should've been able to receive the same kind of transformation just as instantaneously as they did. We think we are hopeless and have gone too far. We weren't honest. We didn't respond and now it's too late. We believe we cannot get free. However, if we continue to speak out and admit those despairing thoughts, they will lessen and eventually go away. If we continue believing and binding together with others, it will come. It may take time and diligent repetition. That is my point. We should not stop trying. There is no end to God's mercy. He is longsuffering. He is kind. He does not give up on us even if we do. Progress is still progress even if it is slow.

I was brought to that place of clarity. As a drunk, we are provided the opportunity to see ourselves in our stupor and God in His mercy. I believe these are God ordained episodes. I was given revelation about my condition several times during those drinking years. It takes deep devastation for some of us to reach complete willingness. Some fellow alcoholics may have listened the first or second time. I did not. I finally gave in to the truth. That was when I began to own my problem. I began to express my need. I needed God and I needed people and I needed help. My change in attitude was the first evidence that I had begun to *speak out*. I was first speaking on the inside before I said it out loud. I finally started to audibly declare, "I'm done. I can't do this. Help! I want out!" This time it was genuine. That is when the light entered the body bag.

Surrender is **spiritual.** I had chosen to live in captivity in the enemy's camp but I did not realize I was making that choice—until it was too late to get out myself. In a sense, we alcoholics and addicts have allowed ourselves to be put in prison. The problem is that we think there is no way out. That is the lie of the enemy. The way out is to *Confess with your mouth and believe in your heart* (Romans 10:9). It's the same act of faith that we perform when we first come to know God. So in essence, if we confess our drunkenness and believe in our heart that we can be saved from it, we will be delivered. That seems too simplistic but spiritual warfare works that way. When we perform a very small prescribed task, we receive an exponentially large return. Our disease wants us to believe that freedom is too complex and unattainable. The only complexity is what happens on the inside of us. We are spiritually transformed. The key is only in the surrendering to God. It takes a small amount of will to say *I give up* but that is all it takes. God does the rest. God changes our mind and will. He gives the desire and the power. It is a miracle of grace.

What was the missing link for me? Why did I continue on for so long? I spent over three years in the *body bag*, trying to get free after I finally wanted it. I believe that the length of time was a result of my failure to expose the lies of this spiritual disease. I hid what the voice of alcoholism was saying in my heart. When I heard "You are hopeless and you will always love alcohol more," I believed it and I did nothing to counteract what I was hearing and thinking. Instead of confessing my fears, I took them in and hid my true thoughts. I would say to others, "Oh, I'm trying. I'm doing everything they told me to do in recovery." I was attempting to work my own way to sobriety but I really didn't believe that I was worthy. I should've first gone to God earnestly, and then to trusted friends and said **HELP! I am stuck in believing that I will never get better and I don't even know if I want to get better!** When I finally began to confess my true thoughts is when I began to see hope.

The fact still remains that I was very loved and accepted by God in the midst of my heaviest drinking. God did not give up on me and He will not give up on others. He is kind. He does not want us to die in addiction.

The answers seem almost too simple: **Affirm the truth**: *I am good and I am forgiven! I can receive help and I can give help to others.* **Dispel lies**: "I reject the lies, *I am hopeless, I am a shameful loser.* I do not receive the lie, *I will never stay sober.* I refuse the lie, *God doesn't* *love me."* Don't quit speaking these truths. We alcoholics need to have other people believe with us that we can get better. I have found that there are many good, helpful people. Those who receive help and those who give help are like a body. The parts of a body are dependent. Recovery groups are a healing body and the Christ-centered church is also a healing body. God helps each body function. The truth is that our freedom was paid for many years ago. We only need to redeem it and receive it. It doesn't matter whether we were already a believer or never a believer. The answers are in fellowship with God and with others who believe. The answers are in honest and open confession. The answers are in forgiving yourself.

*Through the Lord's mercies we are not consumed, because His compassions fail not. They are new every morning; great is Your faithfulness* (Lamentations 3:23).

# CHAPTER
## 24

# SPIRITUAL CONFESSIONS

As I have written my story, I have taken the journey with you. Over the course of five years I have learned many things. I have tried to figure out why I drank. I have stated that I was prideful and certain of my right standing with God. While that is true, I no longer believe it was the cause of my drinking. I have also shared that my failed attempts at sobriety were a spiritual battle that I continued to lose. Though true, that is not the complete picture. The main reason I drank is that I didn't understand God's love and forgiveness. I believe my lack of understanding of His compassion for me is what kept me in bondage to alcohol.

My problem wasn't my behaviors, but my belief. I believed that I was *bad* and my drinking was *bad*. While it is true that my drinking was sinful and *bad*, I have learned that I myself was not *bad*. After all the years of salvation, I was still thinking that I was guilty and condemned every time I drank. God says that I am not under condemnation. Even when I do things wrong, I am loved and forgiven. I am righteous in God's eyes all the time. Otherwise, why did Jesus come? His work on Calvary was not partial. It was complete. He doesn't just love me when I'm obedient or when I am doing good things. He loves me all the time. He doesn't dwell on sin. He sees me as cleansed forever and always.

Some good friends came over to see us shortly after I had been to my first rehab center. Our friend Ray looked at us and said, "Isn't alcoholism a spiritual thing that you are redeemed from?" This question made me feel condemned and angry at the time. I almost stomped off to my bedroom and slammed the door. But now I see that he was sincerely trying to help. Ray was right. The truth was presented to me but I was unable to grasp it. Why? Because deep in my heart I didn't belief in God's full provision. I believed that Christ's payment of forgiveness was for some occasions and not for others. I believed He only forgave good people. I believed His acceptance was tied to my behavior. I misunderstood that the blood of Jesus cleansed me once and for all. When I found out that it was not God that battered me with guilt, I was stunned. All of the years I spent drinking, I was condemning myself alongside the devil. I thought God was mad at me. I thought He was judging me. I thought God wanted to punish me. My constant focus on sin was the problem. I looked at the behaviors instead of at Jesus. Self-condemnation made me only want to drink more, because I was focused on escaping the guilt and rejection. I did not believe that the salvation I had once received still covered my shame. I believed I was saved but just not good enough.

When I truly accepted that God says I am cleansed and righteous **even if I sin**, I no longer wanted to sin. The power to remain free was in knowing that God always sees me as a righteous believer. I thought I had to quit sinning first, but the answer was in knowing He loved me no matter what. That understanding came to me gradually after God called my name in the night at Rayland Road. I had given up. God hadn't. He came to put this truth in my heart.

But there is more to this revelation. Though I knew in my head I shouldn't feel guilty any longer, my heart remained in unbelief. For many of these years of recovery I continued to see myself as shameful, irredeemable, and guilty for my drunken years. This is not what God intended. The shame and guilt were the result of unbelief. I was living far below where God had intended me to live. He desires that I accept His complete love and forgiveness. He desires that I see myself as righteous.

When I realized this, I said a prayer.

*God, I have been living in unbelief of the cross and the forgiveness you gave through Jesus. I confess that I was living as an unbeliever! I didn't value the shed blood of Jesus on the cross. I was still accusing myself of sin when you had already proclaimed me righteous forever. You didn't hold my drinking against me because you had paid for it in full. I repent now and turn from this unbelief of Your full and final payment for my sinful behaviors. Help me walk in agreement with Your great grace and forgiveness. Help me to believe Your word and to stop listening to the lies of the enemy.*

Now that I am starting to grasp this truth, I am no longer struggling with guilt, shame, or the constant nagging of condemnation. I have truly been able to live in freedom. I have learned that He loves me all the time; constantly and always. Forever.

In order to keep my focus right, I make a daily declaration of thanksgiving.

> *Father God, I praise you today for my constant salvation through Jesus. You are my Savior who bought me and who loves me continuously. You see me as cleansed and righteous because of the blood shed by Jesus on my behalf. Thank you, Jesus, for this freedom. Thank you that you do not look at my shortcomings and mistakes, but at the goodness and holiness placed on me by You. I love you and I believe Your love is for me.*

Once I realized this, I received more truths. First, since He forgave me, I forgive me. At first I just spoke the words without feeling them, but it is true now. I forgave me.

Knowing how He sees me has helped me change my view of myself. I am not condemned. I am accepted. I am not guilty. I am free. He paid for my debt and my punishment. My prison sentence and condemnation are cancelled. God wants me to join in with joy and fully receive the total payment that He made. When I live as though I am still guilty, I am behaving as though He did nothing. I cheapen what Jesus did on the cross when I behave as if His suffering is not enough. There are no limits to His forgiveness. Forgiveness is for yesterday, today and the future. His forgiveness is a continuous thing that goes on forever. Nothing is too *bad* or too evil for God's redemption. He knew what I was going to do before I ever did it. He offers peace, joy, forgiveness, and unconditional love. I will accept it. I will believe it.

Because God has compassion for my hurts, He wants me to also have compassion for the hurting places that still remain. His desire is that I experience joy instead of sorrows. I do have compassion now for my own situation. This compassion allows me to see that I was in a state of mental illness for a long time, and I was attempting to escape past, hurtful memories. The compassion I have for other alcoholics, God wants me to have for myself. No more condemnation. I was not evil. I was ill. I was not rebellious. I was emotionally absent. I was not ungrateful. I was wounded. I was not purposely deceitful. I was blinded by pain. These are not excuses. These are merciful truths I never saw before. He alone brought these truths into my unbelieving heart.

God loves the broken. God loves the humiliated. God loves the shamed. He turns it all around and makes it new.

## Prayer of Salvation

If you have never accepted Jesus Christ as your Savior and would like to do so, the following is a prayer that will enable you to come to Him and receive forgiveness and salvation.

*Father God, I come to you now, wanting to know you in a personal way. I confess that I have lived my life by my own selfish motives and sin. I have lived apart from You. I now receive Your forgiveness and Your love. Come into my heart and life and take over. Thank You, Jesus for shedding Your blood for me. I want to live for You now.*

It is important to find a fellowship of believers to join forces with now. This will give you faith to move forward and to learn His Word.

# CHAPTER
## 25

# VISION OF THE FIELD

*I saw a field of green grass and a robed Shepherd. There were hundreds of sheep. Some were grazing. Some ewes were playing and jumping. Many were moving over to the furthest corners of the field to seek shade. As I looked across the grassy pasture, I noticed a gateway with an arch that read,* Enemy's Field. *A few sheep were standing facing that gate, as if in contemplation. I heard the Shepherd call for them to come closer to him. It struck me that there was a group of sheep who surrounded the Good Shepherd. They looked to be in competition for His attention. Some were jumping up to catch His attention. He individually picked up the little sheep and held each one close, gently whispering words of love to each.* "Why do some sheep stay so close?" *I asked. The answer came to me quickly. The sheep that are surrounding the shepherd are those who once strayed through the arch. They were lost but then found again by the Good Shepherd. They were sought out by Him and rescued from the enemy's territory. These redeemed sheep never wish to leave His side again. The memories of being away from Him are too hurtful. It is these sheep who are constantly drawn to receive His love. It is these rescued sheep who have no desire for the other places in the field. It is these who want only His care.*

*It is His grace that rescues these wanderers and His grace alone that keeps them.*

*I had to know why the sheep would go inside the enemy's gate. It made no sense at all.*

*"Why did you go in there?" I asked a returning ewe.*

*I knew the answer myself. The Enemy's gate did not look inviting or scary. That is because I didn't even notice the arch or the letters spelling it out. I only felt the inner drawing of hope for relief. I sought relief of the trauma that ate through my insides. I saw the sparkling cup. It gave immediate oblivion. It gave the hope of lasting joy. Then I heard the enemy laugh. He had deceived me. He gave me notice that I could not return to the Shepherd. The cup was a sign of resignation forever. I might as well go deep, I thought. I don't want to feel that absence from My Lord.*

*The enemy thought he had me now. He thought I was his forever. The white robe blinded him. My rescuer had come. He called my name. He stretched out his hand and said,* **"Come with me. You are lost. You decided to try the enemy's gate. The evil one cannot snatch you out of my hand."**

*"But I went through his gate!" I cried. The Shepherd gently laughed.*

**"You are mine. You belong to me.** *" He picked me up, not with his staff, but with His own hands, and carried me through the gate and back to His pasture.*

*This was the everlasting joy! The enemy's anesthesia had proved worthless and conniving. But suddenly I cowered in shame. How could I have gone with the enemy? The Shepherd knew my thoughts. He picked me up again and said lovingly yet sternly,* **"I paid! I bore your shame. I carried your sorrows. I still carry the shame and sorrows so**

**that you do not have to. You are free."** *When He set me down again, I felt the freedom but I also felt myself drawn. I do not ever want to leave His side. There is nothing else. There is no one else. There is only Him.*

I went far into enemy territory. I tried His grace but I could not exhaust it. It does abound. True grace brings freedom from the want of other things.

## Kerry's Journal, July 2017
### *Looking Back*

*It was not an accident that I arrived at Rayland Road the same time as Frank, who told me everything would be okay. For some reason I believed him. It was not an accident that a therapist picked me to work with his intern who enabled me to heal from past trauma. Nor was it an accident that the "big sister" assigned to me became like a true big sister. It was not an accident that my bunkmate had been a prostitute who helped me see my own pride and ungratefulness. Favor has continually come forward in situations where I had little control or hope of positive outcome. I did not ask for any special treatment. I did not ask for consequences to be removed. But in looking back, I can see a power at work in circumstances that allowed me time, space, and unique favor.*

*But there is more. The psychiatrist at my first treatment happened to be from my own church, and became instrumental in helping my husband. Another teacher came to my house and broke her own anonymity to help and encourage me. Dr. Gibbs, a "substitute" psychiatrist for my therapy session, led me into a moment of clarity that changed my mind and will about long-term treatment. A kind woman, Marg, who later became my sponsor, approached me at my first recovery meeting and asked if she could help me. I was given an amazingly compatible roommate during my fragile time of three quarter house living. When it was time to look for temporary work in the city, I received the desired position for which I interviewed. A student nominated me for the "Make a Difference Award" during the time I was on leave for rehab. A merciful decision was made by my school district that it was best for **all** to offer me leave, rehabilitation, contractual guidelines, and accountability testing. A board member who was known to be hard and critical, kindly encouraged me and asked what I needed during my transition. There were two separate grandparents of my students who hugged me every time I saw them. I was able to maintain a job I loved without which I would have had little incentive to stop drinking. Odds were favorable that I would experience arrest and jail time for driving under the influence, but I never received those well-deserved consequences. My husband and youngest son, who to some seemed like enablers, were there to lovingly let* *me know that I was not going to make it on my own. The same was true of my church, my friends, my family, my coworkers, and even parents of many students. Though I had proven untrustworthy, they stood by me. People still believed in me!*

*I call it grace. I was shown unmerited favor by God and, consequently, by people. I now see a single strand of thread connecting every situation in which I found myself. It was not by any human effort, but often by the actions of willing people who were directed according to the will of God's invisible thread. These efforts were contrary to human reasoning or understanding. No one cut me slack or looked the other way. These individuals were showing me grace. Most did not realize their involvement. The kindness and undeserved mercy of both God and man was demonstrated to me. This was true graciousness. At the time, I was either unaware of these actions, or in many circumstances, I did not appreciate the loving favor shown me.*

*Why me? I certainly did not deserve it. I deserved consequences. There seems to be two answers. The first is simple but very true; I belonged to God. He responds to His people with mercy whenever possible. The second, people were praying for me. Many people were interceding for my safety and restoration. Now I am grateful beyond words. I knew some of these praying people, but many I still do not know. God has shown me that the faith of these believing friends is what He used to turn my situation around. My will was changed but I didn't do it.*

*I am saying all this now because I hope you see this hand of God. I hope you can recognize His merciful kindness as I do now. I hope you notice the thread that weaves the circumstances and situations together. I hope you feel His presence and hear His truth. He is a God who rescues and restores. He is a God who brings hope to broken, ravaged lives. He is a God who loves no matter what. He is a God who doesn't give up on us or turn His back when others would. He is a God who loves mercy.*

# KERRY'S EPILOGUE

I didn't know who I was.

Even though I was saved, I thought I was shameful because I was a drunken Christian. I thought I was eternally inferior, though I had once been redeemed. I thought I might not make it to heaven because I had proven to be unfit. Most importantly, I thought that God had given up on me. I even believed He wanted to punish me.

I was a believer who did not believe some important truths about God and the salvation He provided.

The truth is I am forgiven now and forever. I am accepted today and forever—no matter what. When I criticize me, I am criticizing God's plan of salvation.

I used to believe that the first goal of Christianity was to clean up my behavior, and then stay away from sin. That made me all the more conscious of my shortcomings and my failure to stay sober. It kept me harboring resentment about my lack of obedience. I was conscious only of my drunkenness. Trying to be good stole my desire and power to live in the intended outcome of freedom. Trying to earn my way wiped out the understanding of being cleansed from my sin. I was stuck in the habit of recording and replaying my sin, and trying to figure out what to do about it. This is the intent of the evil one. He delights in getting Christians to feel condemned when we are convinced that our own efforts are not good enough. Unfortunately, I believed the condemnation. I owned it.

I found out that by keeping my attention on my *Rescuer*, I finally wanted to stop drinking. By looking at my *Rescuer*, not at myself, I could change. By listening to my *Rescuer*, I could love and accept myself. That had to happen before I could get sober; I had to love the old me, the *icky* me. Jesus, my Rescuer did that. If He could love me while I was in the body bag, then I could love me too. If He could enter the enemy's gate to go after me, one lost sheep, then I could see my worth too. If He called out my name in the night *after* I admitted I wanted to go drink again, than I can forgive me too.

I am not a prisoner after all. Jesus makes the way for my continued victory and walk of faith. I am not drinking anymore because I don't *want* to. I don't *want* to drink because I've changed. I've changed because I know I'm loved and favored. I'm loved and favored because of the mercy of God and the grace of Jesus Christ. I didn't get free by being good. I didn't get free by doing good. I'm not good because I'm sober. I'm good because He bought me. He ransomed me when I was a drunken hypocrite.

I wish I had known who I was sooner. That's why I wrote this book. I want to spread the word to others in addiction that our Rescuer, Jesus, who was the substitute for our addiction, changes us. He continues to be our substitute forever. We don't pay for our own sin. We don't clean ourselves up. He does it all. All are rescued. He never leaves or forsakes those who are His.

I know who I am now because I know who He is.

"Let the redeemed of the Lord say so,
Whom He has redeemed
From the hand of the enemy" (Psalm 107:2).

"But where sin abounded, grace abounded much more" (Romans 5:20).

"He brought me up out of a horrible pit,
Out of the miry clay,
And set my feet upon a rock,
And established my steps.
He has put a new song in my mouth—
Praise to our God
Many will see it and fear,
And will trust in the Lord" (Psalm 40:2–3).

# RICK'S EPILOGUE

I have a confession. I never wanted this project. I wasn't thrilled by the thought of airing our life in the pages of a memoir. When Kerry approached me about sharing our story, at first, I rendered tacit ascent. I nodded, smiled, and hoped it would go away. To be honest, I didn't believe she'd do it. But when she started to actually write the thing, I forced myself into passive interest fueled by procrastination. I didn't want her to write it. And I sure as hell didn't want to tell my story.

For one thing, I was embarrassed. I was ashamed of how stupid I was; first, for not even noticing her addiction; later, for not knowing how to fix it; but mostly, for how utterly helpless and overwhelmed I was in the face of this monster of a disease that grew way too big for me to wrestle.

This was not me at my best. It was not a story that painted me in the best light.

But gradually my shame became my motivation. For my shame was shared by every husband, wife, parent, sibling, child, friend of an addict. My shame needed to be exposed to assure others that their shame was not only shared but was common. It was a shame borne of fear. I was staring at a giant, day in and day out, armed only with a sling and a stone. But I was no David. I'd never killed a bear or a lion. I'd never faced anything this frightening, this huge, this overwhelmingly powerful. I was untrained and unfit for battle. And everyone I loved, everyone I knew was looking to me to kill the giant. And it had to be done. This giant had to die. Because this giant held my wife in his grip. And if he didn't die, and die soon, she would certainly die.

I penned my part for the sake of those like me standing alone in the arena and facing their giant whose grip on someone they love was reducing them to hopelessness, helplessness, and utter despair. And though my despair came from believing I must kill the giant, the fact was, Kerry's freedom rested in the key she herself gripped. As the giant gripped her, she gripped the key to the shackles that held her. I grew to learn that even if I was able the kill the beast, she would remain shackled to its body until she could muster the courage to unshackle herself. There was no other way. I had no key. Nor did anyone else. It remained in her hand. It remained her decision.

I have no magic potion for how to free your wife. I have no recipe for releasing your husband from this brutal beast. I have no key, nor do you. The key will always remain in the hands of the addict. When you stay close to the addict, you stay close to the beast. And if they choose to remain bound, those they love can be subject to an ugly, even dangerous life. He is a mean SOB and we're standing within range. He's unkind, yells obscenities, spits, and throws things. Sometimes shrapnel flies. Sometimes you get hurt. And you must choose. If you stay, there's a chance that you can coax the addict to use their key. Yet staying is risky. And if you have others with you, small children, they're at risk as well. If you leave, there's a chance your addict may follow. Like the toddler kicking a tantrum in the store aisle, there's a chance that walking away will awaken your addict to the reality that getting up and following is better than remaining alone. But they might not follow. They might stay and die in the grip of the beast. And you're the one who left them there. Or you're the fool who chose to live in chaos. You're damned if you do and damned if you don't.

So you come seeking certainty. You come longing for guaranteed success. The only certainty I offer is this. Regardless of your decision, you have no promise of success. Whatever choice you make, you will be criticized. But I won't criticize. Nor will I call you a fool. Nor will any of us who have faced the same giant. Some of us won. Some lost. Some stayed. Some left. Ours is not a story of valor. Ours is not a story of guaranteed success.

I chose to stay. Not because I'm brave or noble or godly. Not as a therapy exercise to trick her into recovery, but simply because I loved her. I loved her then when she was drunk. I love her now, twelve years sober. And if she drinks tomorrow, I will continue to love her. It's something I can't change. Nor is it a testimony to my nobility or courage. It is rather evidence of the move of God in my being. It is my testimony. It is my truth. And regardless of Kerry's sobriety, He remains my hope. I will not spend this time justifying my ability to know God and hear His voice. That's another book. I instead lay it before you as my solace. And I offer it before you as your hope. God's voice is a gift that you can share.

It's not about staying. Nor is it about leaving. It's about hearing God. It's about praying fervently. It's about believing He hears me and listens with interest and love. And it's about believing He responds to what I say.

Ours is a story of hope. But without God there is no hope. Resting on our own capacity to overcome this deadly disease, we will win only by shear chance. Our skills, insights, intellect, determination, personal fortitude may chance upon success, but more likely yield repeated frustration.

So here's my message. Here's my proposal. Here's my counsel to what I've found to be the best, if not the only path to sanity.

Pray.

*Really, Rick?*

Yes, really. I know you have prayed. And I'm here to tell you to continue, placing your faith, trust, and hope in Him. Pray with eyes and ears open, expecting—demanding—answers. I'm not telling you to not use people. Use people. Use the therapists. Use the psychiatrists. Use the physicians and rehab centers and techniques and self-help books. Use Al Anon. Use all the experts. But BELIEVE God. Put your hope in God. Put your hope in prayer. Put your hope in the only One who can change hearts. And be open to the possibility that it may not be the addict's heart He wishes to change, but yours.

Don't misunderstand. I am NOT telling you to change your attitude under your own power. You hurt, you worry, you might even hate. That is real. You have no more capacity to transform yourself than you do to transform your addict. What I am saying is be ready for the possibility that God may choose to change your heart. By that I mean, He can be your closest friend and confidant, and He may just have something to say that will impact what you do and how you act.

When we are in the battle for as long as some of us have been engaged, we begin to stop feeling—or at least avoid feeling. Because the only feelings we know are hurt. But if you pray for God to awaken a change in you, He has the ability to reveal His truth—truth about His love for you—truth about His love for your addict. And it is that truth that has the power to awaken new beliefs, new realities, that lead to new feelings.

All I'm saying is this. Let God speak to Your heart. Let Him change what you believe. Let Him change what you feel. He knows things you never knew. He remembers things you've long forgotten or buried deep within. What you feel is heavy. He wants to lift that heaviness.

I want to promise you life. I can offer you hope and sanity. When we choose to love someone, anyone, we risk pain. The best of us disappoint. When we choose to love an addict, we can be assured of pain. But don't let others shame you for your choice, or shame you into choosing *their* next step rather than the step that God has in store for you. Don't let others demean the one you chose to love. It is never foolish to love. Nor is it foolish to love someone when they are broken, sick, unattractive, or selfish. God has a way of reminding us of when we were loved in the midst of our brokenness, sickness, unattractiveness, or selfishness. Perhaps it was by someone who now finds themself broken and needing love.

You are reading this because you love, and it hurts. You want the hurt to stop. You ask, *Can I change their hurtful behavior? Can I keep them from hurting me?*

You can't change their hurtful behavior. Sometimes they get sober. But that doesn't always change the hurtful behavior. But even if they recover, know that relapse happens. My wife relapsed repeatedly, finding her longest sobriety (twelve years at the time of this writing) in her eighth rehab facility. It happens when they decide it happens, and not when you decide.

*Can I keep them from hurting me?* You can mitigate the pain. You can take care of yourself, and those you look out for. You can take care of your needs and allow your addict to take care of theirs. You can let them face the consequences that result from their addiction. I found support and strength through Al-Anon. I strongly recommend reading *How Al-Anon Works*, *Courage to Change*, and *Alcoholics Anonymous*. It is important to arm yourself with knowledge of this disease as well as the insight and council of those who have lived it. You may find through prayer and study you still love your addict. You may learn otherwise. Just know that your course of action is yours and yours alone. No one can tell you how to best follow God's path for own recovery, nor what personal decision may best impact your addict's recovery. Know only that God's deep love for you and your addict, and your children, will guide your decisions and render you hope.

Know that God listens. And know that God speaks.

# LETTER TO THE CHURCH

D<small>ear</small> Church,

I would like to tell you what happened to me the day I came back to church after returning from rehab for alcoholism. A sister in Christ that I knew slightly came up to me. She stood only a few feet away. She was staring directly into my eyes. I was immediately filled with fear. *Oh no. Here it comes. I knew judgment would be here.* She opened her mouth and proclaimed "I love you, I love you, I love you!" Then she warmly hugged me. This stayed with me all day. No, it stayed with me all week. No, all year—even all decade. It is still with me now.

I don't know if you realize the impact you have on someone who is returning to church from an addiction. If you love, there is explosive far reaching impact of glory. If you judge, you foster condemnation that spreads like a wild fire. If you do nothing, it is felt as apathy. It is a dismissal.

The meaning of *the returning* may not be obvious. The sister or brother who is returning is coming back with uncertainty about how the church will respond. They were likely carried in the door by the Savior Himself. They know He loves. Will the church love as He does? Please don't feel shy or embarrassed about greeting us. This *returning one* has already been through loss, shame, and condemnation. Fear is most likely raging. They don't want space; they want unconditional love and acceptance. If you can't give this, than please try pretending and ask the Holy Spirit to help you with this.

Beware of the prowling enemy who may be whispering, *But they can't just come back in here and act like nothing happened!*

Something **has** happened. A breaking happened. This returning Christian is wading through the debris.

Consequences have been experienced because of addiction. Some of the natural consequences are distrust, poverty, broken marriages and families, loneliness, physical and emotional illness, low self-worth, shame, loss of honor and position. If a believer has fallen, there are also consequences related to our Christian walk; we've lost faith in God and His Word; we seek restoration when there is little hope of remaining options; there may be uncertainty about salvation; will we have right standing in the church? We may feel that we have lost all reward for previous Christian service. We wonder if we have any friends remaining.

There are deep spiritual consequences for those who have been in addiction. We still have our wounds that led us to the addiction in the first place. We have the great need to get free of these. We look for help from the body of Christ. We may feel that our spiritual gifts burned up like the field of briars because of our disloyalty to God. We fight with regret, depression, and disappointment and many other lies from the enemy. We especially wrestle with fear of the enemy because he won the last time. It is a complete over haul that is needed. But God is able if we are willing to seek His help and the body's. We who are returning are not irredeemable.

Lastly, there are evil consequences planted by the enemy. Humans who partner with the enemy are a major part of this. We *returners* may continue to be shunned. We *rightly* feel ashamed. We may be judged unworthy of the name of Christ Jesus. Eyes roll. Backs turn when we talk about his great grace. We are in the fellowship but not of the fellowship. We hear that it is said that we *abused His grace. I suppose that he will go drink again!*

Does grace run out? Whose grace is it? It is **His** hard earned grace. Jesus bought each of us with His own blood. He can do with His grace as He pleases and He pleases to let us know that *WHERE SIN ABOUNDS, GRACE ABOUNDS MUCH MORE.* Grace actually **is** a *license.* It is a license to receive unmerited favor and mercy. Yes! But now that I know this, do I want to sin? Absolutely not. NO. It is backward. I stayed away **because** I didn't know his grace. It is not about the sinning. It is about the receiving. There is no limit on God's gifts of forgiveness and mercy. That's why He came.

He took us back. He keeps us close. We will not let go. He will not let go. We who are returning need to experience the same acceptance from the body of Christ that we received from God. We need to know that we will not be abandoned by our church.

There is lack of communication about addictions in the church. Most of us who were saved, and then fell into habitual sin, had deep inner wounds that we could not get free of. That signals the enemy, who is prowling about, with a huge invitation. He offers an escape from pain. In no way am I excusing sin or creating a loophole for backsliding. I am merely pointing out that we did not understand grace because our pain did not allow us to receive. Wounded people cannot easily receive. We can receive salvation because that is a one-time provision of faith. But to receive the grace to walk in freedom is not as easy to grasp. All of our energy is wrapped up in our pain. That is why once our pain takes us to the bottom of the pit of despair, we finally awaken to truth. We have been rescued. We can see it clearly now. The realization of His great mercy transforms us. Some of us had to experience that leaving and returning so that the vastness of true love could be experienced. I was given supernatural appreciation when He called my name. Grace breeds more grace. Now I have also been freed from the wounds. Grace upon grace brings more freedom.

I believe that God desires to heal these misunderstandings of grace in church. Legalism has told people in recovery that their standing is different and they may have to earn their way back. If they left the fold, they may be subtly told that they cannot make it back. If they left the fellowship to follow sin, they lost their salvation.

I am not a preacher so I won't try and teach about this. I can pray though, and God has told me to pray that the church does not get caught in the enemy's snare concerning addiction;

*Dear Father, I pray that those who judge the returning addicts will turn from their judgment and criticism. I pray the church will receive the rain of grace and mercy. I cry out for overcoming victory over this criticism, self-righteousness, and pride in the name of the Lord Jesus Christ. I declare Grace, grace and more grace to these divisions and resentments on both sides of this issue. God, deliver us from this evil plan of the enemy to divide and destroy the church. Please have mercy on the church for turning their back. Turn hearts back to you.*

*Bring us into one fold. Bring us into holy unity. Amen.*

God bless you.
Kerry

CPSIA information can be obtained
at www.ICGtesting.com
Printed in the USA
FFHW020320160119
50188197-55153FF